Praxis® II Early Childhood Education (5025)

How to pass the Praxis® 5025 by using effective test prep, proven strategies, practice test questions, and relevant examples.

Kathleen Jasper LLC
Estero, FL 33928
http://www.kathleenjasper.com | info@KathleenJasper.com

Praxis® 5025 Early Childhood Education: How to pass the Praxis® 5025 by using effective test prep, proven strategies, practice test questions, and relevant examples.

Printed in the United States of America
ISBN: 9798700737210

I'm Kathleen Jasper, and for the last decade, I've been helping prospective teachers and school leaders pass their certification exams and get the positions they want in education. To date, I've helped over 80,000 educators on their certification journeys.

I've had many positions in public education. I started off as a substitute teacher and went through the certification process you are going through right now. I was hired as a high school reading and biology teacher, and a couple of years later had the opportunity to work in curriculum at the district office. Finally, I became a high school assistant principal.

I left public education to start my own company, Kathleen Jasper LLC, and now I write study guides, conduct online courses, create content, and more to help you pass your exams and land your desired position.

I am thrilled you're here. Thank you for taking the time to review my content and purchase my products. It means the world to me to help educators all over the country.

Would you mind leaving a review?

Did you purchase this book on Amazon? If so, I would be thrilled if you would leave an unbiased review at your convenience. Did you purchase this book from kathleenjasper.com? If so, you can leave a review on Facebook, Google, or directly on our website on the product page. Thank you so much.

Check out my other products.

I have built several comprehensive, self-paced online courses for many teacher certification exams. I also have other books, webinars, and more. Go to https://kathleenjasper.com/ and use offer code **EARLY10** for 10% off any of my products.

If you have any questions, don't hesitate to reach out to info@kathleenjasper.com. It will be my pleasure to help. Good luck with your exam.

– Kathleen Jasper, Ed.D.

Follow me on social media.   @kathleenjasperEdD   @kathleen_jasper

 KathleenJasperEdD   @kj_kathleenjasper   @kathleenjasper

This page intentionally left blank.

Table of Contents

How to Use this Book

We value the importance and necessity of great teachers; without you, many children's futures would be at risk. Nothing can replace enthusiastic, well-prepared teachers who love their craft and who want to pass their knowledge and passion onto others. It is our mission to prepare learners for success. We build materials that will help you achieve on your certification exams.

How to study

This book was developed using the test specifications provided in the ETS Praxis® Early Childhood Education (5025) Study Companion. All of the skills covered in this book come directly from the test blueprint provided in that document. As with all of our study guides, we strongly recommend test takers thoroughly review the test blueprint provided by the test maker. We reference the information in the Praxis® Early Childhood Education (5025) test blueprint throughout this book which can be found at this link: https://www.ets.org/s/praxis/pdf/5025.pdf.

It is our recommendation that you take the time to read through the entire book. We have worked as teachers, school-level administrators, and district-level administrators, so we know what is expected of teachers from the school, the district, and the state. We have used this knowledge to prepare a comprehensive study guide that will give you the tools, tips, and resources to be successful on your certification exam and in your classroom.

If you only have a short amount of time to prepare for your exam, take a practice test at the end of each content category in the book. Use the answer explanations provided after each practice test to determine what competencies and skills you may still need to master and read through those sections of the book. After reading through specific content categories, work through the practice test to assess your mastery of the material.

Tips, tricks, and strategies

We understand that not every new teacher is knowledgeable in all the content and subskills assessed on the Praxis® 5025. Therefore, we've worked diligently to study the test blueprint and sample items to provide you with strategies and tips for navigating through questions on concepts you may encounter on the exam.

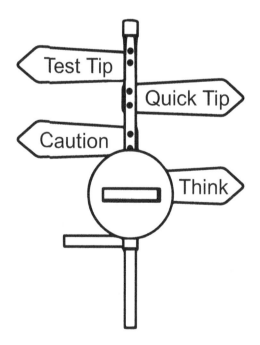

Our materials are designed to get you through all of the skills on this exam as quickly and painlessly as possible. We focus only on the skills you need to be successful. We also share the shortcuts and strategies that will get you that passing score, even if you're not confident in taking standardized exams.

Throughout the book, we highlight various tips and strategies. We've broken them down into four categories and identify them by icons. Use key that follows to help you understand each type of tip we provide.

QUICK TIPS: These tips are represented with a megaphone and include tips and vocabulary you need to know or strategies for answering questions for a particular skill or content category.

 TEST TIPS: Test tips are represented with a light bulb and are specific test taking strategies that can be, and should be, used while taking the exam.

 THINK ABOUT IT: These tips are not necessarily tested concepts, but they provide background information to help make sense of concepts and give necessary information to help answer questions on the exam.

 CAUTION: Caution tips explain what to avoid when selecting your answer choices on the exam. Test writers are very good at creating distracting answer choices that seem like good options. We teach you what to watch for when it comes to distractors, so you avoid these pitfalls.

Book organization

The sections of the book are arranged by the 5 content categories of the Praxis® 5025. In addition, each content category is broken down by skill. The book mirrors the skills outlined in the Praxis® 5025 Study Companion. Within each of the skill sections are examples and explanations of what you need to know to be successful on the exam.

Extra practice

We know you want extra practice problems to work on your skills. Therefore, at the end of each content category we include 10 additional practice problems. These are problems on top of the full practice test at the end of the book. Use these extra practice problems to determine if you have a firm grasp on each of the content category. If you do not get at least 7 of the extra practice problems correct (70%), revisit the content category.

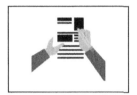

Practice test

There is one full practice test at the end of the book. Questions and answer explanations are organized by content category, so you can see where you have strengths and where you have weaknesses. Use the ten-question quizzes at the end of each content category as a pretest to measure your current capabilities in that area. Look over the content category in which you are weak. Then, after reading and working through all the sections and example problems, take the practice test. Use this test to monitor your progress. Mark areas where you may still need improvement, and go back and study those skills.

Quick reference guides

We have included a reference guide at the end of the book. There you will find our good words/bad words list, classroom assessments table, and classroom strategies and practices. This is all information you will most likely encounter on the exam, so don't skip this part of the book. Use the information in the reference guide to **_think like a test maker, not a test taker_**.

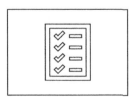

About the Test

The Praxis® Early Childhood Education (5025) exam is designed to assess standards-based knowledge of skills and competencies of prekindergarten to third grade teachers. The assessment is comprised of 5 content categories. The following table provides a blueprint of the assessment.

Test at a Glance	
Test Name	Early Childhood Education
Test Code	5025
Time	2 hours
Number of Questions	120
Format	Selected Response
Test Delivery	Computer delivered

Content Category	Approx. Number of Questions	Approx. Percentage of Exam
I. Language and Literacy	36	30%
II. Mathematics	30	25%
III. Social Studies	17	14%
IV. Science	17	14%
V. Health and Physical Education; Creative and Performing Arts	20	17%

I. Language and Literacy

A – Emergent Literacy: Foundational Skills

1. Stages of language acquisition
2. Instruction for all students with diverse needs
3. Print Awareness
4. The role of phonological awareness in literacy development

1. Stages of language acquisition

Readers at the emergent literacy stage are learning to read and understand words by decoding the reading process as they engage with the text. Emergent literacy involves the skills, knowledge, and attitudes that are developmental precursors to conventional forms of reading and writing (Whitehurst & Lonigan, 1998). Emergent literacy skills begin developing in early infancy and early childhood through participation with adults in meaningful activities involving speaking and reading.

Oral language development

Oral language consists of 6 major areas: phonology, vocabulary, morphology, grammar, pragmatics, and discourse.

- **Phonology** encompasses the organization of sounds in language.
- **Vocabulary** (semantics) encompasses both expressive (speaking) and receptive (listening) vocabulary.
- **Morphology** is the study of word structure. Morphemes are the smallest units of meaning words. For example, students use prefixes, suffixes and roots to derive meaning. In the word *unbelievable*, there are three morphemes: *un* (not), *believe*, and *able.*
- **Grammar** (syntax) is the structure of language and words.
- **Pragmatics** focuses on the social cues or norms in language. This is often referred to as situations in language.
- **Discourse** focuses on speaking and listening skills in language.

Written Language Development

As students learn to read, they use different processes to decode words and develop their skills. As they develop their skills, they also evolve through different stages of word recognition.

Stages of word recognition

Students learn to decode their reading by breaking down words in a variety of ways. The initial stage of decoding occurs through the following phases of word recognition: pre-alphabetic, partial-alphabetic, full-alphabetic, and consolidated alphabetic (Ehri, 1999).

▼ **Pre-Alphabetic Phase**
Students read words by memorizing visual features or guessing words from context.

▼ **Partial-Alphabetic Phase**
Students recognize some letters and can use them to remember words by sight.

▼ **Full-Alphabetic Phase**
Readers possess extensive working knowledge of the graphophonemic system, and they can use this knowledge to analyze fully the connections between graphemes and phonemes in words. They can decode unfamiliar words and store fully analyzed sight words in memory.

▼ **Consolidated-Alphabetic Phase**
Students consolidate their knowledge of grapheme-phoneme blends into larger units that recur in different words.

Spelling conventions are the rules that English words follow. Common spelling conventions are found in the following two tables.

The following table includes examples of how teachers and students can use letter sound correspondence, spelling conventions, and graphemes to teach literacy. This information was adapted from the Common Core State Standards for English Language Arts and Literacy Appendix A.

Grapheme Type	Definition	Examples
Single letters	A single consonant letter can be represented by a phoneme.	b, d, f, g, h, j, k, l, m, n, p, r, s, t, v, w, y, z
Doublets	A doublet uses two of the same letter to spell a consonant phoneme.	ff, ll, ss, zz
Digraphs	Digraphs are a two-letter (di-) combinations that create one phoneme.	th, sh, ch, wh, ph, ng (sing) gh (cough) ck
Trigraphs	Trigraphs are three-letter (tri-) combinations that create one phoneme.	-tch -dge
Diphthong	Diphthongs are sounds formed by the combination of two vowels in a single syllable, in which the sound begins as one vowel and moves toward another. They can appear in the initial, middle or final position in a word.	aisle coin loud

Grapheme Type	Definition	Examples
Consonant blends	Consonant blends include two or three graphemes, and the consonant sounds are separate and identifiable.	s-c-r (scrape) c-l (clean) l-k (milk)
Silent letter combinations	Silent letter combinations use two letters: one represents the phoneme and the other is silent.	kn (knock) wr (wrestle) gn (gnarl)
Combination *qu*	These two letters always go together and make a /kw/ sound.	**qu**ickly
Single letters	A single vowel letter that stands for a vowel sound.	(short vowels) cat, hit, gem, pot, sub (long vowels) me, no, mute
Vowel teams	Vowel teams are combinations of two, three, or four letters that stand for a vowel sound.	(short vowels) head, hook (long vowels) boat, rain, weigh (diphthongs) soil, bout

(Appendix A – Common Core State Standards)

The following table outlines rules students must know during the emergent phase of literacy.

Rule	Example
The letter *k* before *e, i,* or *y* makes a /k/ sound.	kite, key
The letter *c* before *a, o, u,* or any consonant makes a /k/ sound.	cat, cost, cut, clap
When *c* is followed by an *e, i,* or *y*, it makes an /s/ sound.	cycle, receive
The letter *q* is always followed by a *u*.	queen, quick
English words don't end in *i; y* is used instead.	my, fly
Use *ck* at the end of one-syllable words after a short vowel.	luck, tuck, stuck
Usually, *k* comes after two consonants or a long vowel sound.	look, skunk, book
When *c* comes at the end of a two or more-syllable word, it makes a /k/ sound.	garli**c**, Atlanti**c**
Always follow *k* with an *e* following a long vowel sound at the end of the word.	like, strike, hike, make

Rule	Example
The letters *ss, ff, ll* are often doubled at the end of a one-syllable word that ends with that sound.	floss, fluff, chill
i before *e* except after *c*, except as in *neighbor* and *weigh*. Exception - when *c* is making an /*sh*/ sound.	receive, believe ancient, glacier
The letter *g* before *e, i,* or *y* sounds like /*j*/.	gel, giant, gym
The letter *g* followed by any other letter sounds like /*g*/.	glass, grow, get

2. Instruction for all students with diverse needs

First language (L1) acquisition refers to the way children learn their native language. Second language (L2) acquisition refers to the learning of another language or languages besides the native language. Typically, language acquisition is associated with English language learners (ELLs).

Below are the stages an ELL goes through during second language acquisition.

Stage	Description
Stage 1: Pre-Production	This is commonly known as the silent period. At this stage, students are listening and deciphering vocabulary. Students may have receptive vocabulary (listening), but they are not speaking yet. In this stage, students benefit from repetition when trying to understand new words and phrases.
Stage 2: Early Production	This stage can last up to six months. Students at this stage understand about 1000 words in the new language. Students begin to form short phrases that may be grammatically incorrect. Students at this stage will use pictures to represent ideas in the new language.
Stage 3: Speech Emergence	At this stage, students will start to communicate with simple phrases and sentences. Students understand up to 3000 words during this stage. Students also begin to develop comprehension in the new language (L2).
Stage 4: Intermediate Fluency	During this stage, students have a robust vocabulary in the second language—6000 or more words. Students begin to communicate effectively in their writing and speech.
Stage 5: Advanced Fluency	At this stage, students are proficient and have comprehension and critical thinking in the second language. It can take 4–10 years for students to achieve academic proficiency in a second language.

Test Tip

ELLs in the early stages of second language acquisition benefit from visual representations. Therefore, if there is a choice to use pictures to accommodate and help ELLs in the pre-production or early production stages, it's probably the correct answer.

World-class Instructional Design and Assessment (WIDA) – WIDA is an organization that supports multilingual students and creates standards and assessments to help with the instruction of ELLs. WIDA supports students, families, educators, and administrators with research-based tools and resources.

The WIDA framework includes five components that are interactive and interdependent. These components exemplify the WIDA vision for academic language development.

1. Guiding Principles of Language Development
2. Developmentally Appropriate Academic Language in Sociocultural Contexts
3. Performance Definitions
4. Can Do descriptors
5. Standards Matrices

Students with special needs and gifted and talented students

In all literacy instruction, it is important for teachers to accommodate students to meet the needs of every learner. Teachers do this by differentiation and modification. For students with special needs, perhaps accommodations are needed like extra time, or larger print, depending on the disability. For students who are gifted and talented, differentiation may mean a more complex piece of text, or a way for the students to extend the learning. Either way, the teacher must accommodate students through differentiation and meeting the specific needs of every student.

3. Print Awareness

Print awareness refers to a child's understanding of the nature and uses of print. Children develop print awareness when they can recognize words as distinct elements of oral and written communication. Both skills are acquired in the child's natural environment.

Environmental print is the print of everyday life. It is the name given to the print that appears on signs, labels, and logos. Street signs, candy wrappers, labels on peanut butter and cereal boxes are other examples of environmental print.

Print concepts involve understanding the difference between letters, words, punctuation and directionality. Print concepts foster reading comprehension and vocabulary growth. Print concepts include:

- **Directionality** – reading from left to right and top to bottom
- **Layout** – front and back of books
- **Differentiation** – words vs pictures and letters vs words

Caution

Avoid answer choices that describe silent independent reading. Usually on the exam, independent reading will be attached to a scenario where a student is struggling. If a student is struggling, the student needs support, and independent reading does not provide support.

4. The role of phonological awareness in literacy development

Phonological awareness is an overarching skill that includes identifying and manipulating units of oral language, including parts of words, syllables, onsets, and rimes.

Children who have phonological awareness are able to:

- Identify and make oral rhymes,

- Clap out the number of syllables in a word,

- Recognize words with the same initial sounds as in *monkey* and *mother*,

- Recognize the sound of spoken language,

- Blend sounds together (*bl, tr, sk*), and

- Divide and manipulate words.

1. **Phonemic awareness** is understanding the individual sounds (or phonemes) in words. For example, students who have phonemic awareness can separate the sounds in the word *cat* into three distinct phonemes: /k/, /æ/, and /t/.

2. **Phonics** is understanding the relationship between sounds and spelling patterns (graphemes) representing those sounds. For example, when a student sees a *c* followed by an *e, i,* or *y*, the student knows the *c* makes an /s/ sound, as in the words *cycle, circle,* and *receive*. The student associated the letters with the appropriate sound.

Phonemic Awareness	Phonics
Focus on phonemes/sounds only	Focus on graphemes/letters and their corresponding sounds
Spoken language	Written language/print
Mostly auditory	Both visual and auditory
Manipulating sounds in words	Reading and writing letters according to sounds, spelling, patterns, and phonological structure

Phonemic awareness activities

There are several ways to implement phonemic awareness in the classroom. On the exam, you will probably see phonemic awareness presented in the following ways.

- **Rhyming** – Matching sounds in words, usually the endings.

- **Segmentation** – Breaking a word apart by phonemes—/b/a/t/.

- **Isolation** – When students isolate a single sound in the word. For example, if the teacher says, "say only the first sound in bat." The students reply with /b/.

- **Deletion** – When students take words apart, remove one sound, and pronounce the word without the removed sound (Caldwell, Jennings, & Lerner, 2014). For example, using the word mice, a teacher may ask students to delete the initial /m/ sound, resulting in the word *ice*. This skill is usually practiced orally.

- **Substitution** – When students replace one sound with another in a word. For example, substitute the first sound in the word cat with an /s/ sound. Students say *sat*.

- **Blending** – The ability to string together the sounds that each letter stands for in a word. For example, when students hear the word black, they blend the /bl/, the /a/ sound, and the ending /k/ sound. Sometimes blending exercises focus just on the consonant blend, like the /br/ sound in the word brick.

Students can break words down to even smaller pieces by focusing on letter sound relationships. For example, Words can be broken down by:

Quick Tip

Think of phonological awareness as the umbrella encompassing many skills students need for literacy: syllabication, onsets, rimes, spelling, etc. Phonemic awareness and phonics are the subskills under the umbrella that support phonological awareness.

- inflected forms (*-s, -es, -ed, -ing, -ly*)

- contractions

- possessives

- compound words

- syllables

- base words

- root words

- prefixes

- suffixes beginning consonants

- end consonants

- medial consonants

- consonant blends (*bl, gr, sp*)

- consonant digraphs (*sh, th, ch*)

- short vowels

- long vowels

- vowel pairs (*oo, ew, oi, oy*)

Blending is an important skill beginners use to mimic the process readers go through to sound out a word as in /p/-/a/-/t/ /pat/.

- **Onsets.** Beginning consonant and consonant cluster.

- **Rimes.** Vowel and consonants that follow. Some common rimes are: *-ack, -an, -aw, -ick, -ing, -op, -unk, -ain, -ank, -ay, -ide, -ink, -or, -ock, -ight, -ame, -eat, -ine*.

Onset / Train / Rime

Chunking

Chunking is a reading activity that involves breaking down a difficult text into manageable pieces. For example, students can read each sentence of a lengthy paragraph. The teacher can break up the paragraph into its individual sentences and have students focus on one sentence at a time.

This page intentionally left blank.

B – Reading: Foundational Skills

1. The role of phonics and word analysis in literacy development
2. The role of fluency in literacy development

1. The role of phonics and word analysis in literacy development

Phonics is a method for teaching children how to read and write by demonstrating the relationship between the sounds of the spoken language, a nd the letters or groups of letters or syllables of the written language. Phonics is essentially spelling.

Syllable Pattern	Description	Example
CVC	consonant-vowel-consonant	bat, cat, tap
CVCe	consonant-vowel-consonant-silent *e*	make, take, bake
CCVC	consonant-consonant-vowel-consonant	trap, chop, grit
CVCC	consonant-vowel-consonant-consonant	tack, hunt, fast
VC-CV	Two or more consonants between two vowels	nap-kin pen-ny
Consonant blend	Consonant blends are stuck together	spec-<u>tr</u>um

Quick Tip

Irregularly Spelled Words

Along with spelling rules, early childhood teachers must help students understand that not all words follow established spelling rules. For example, in the word *said*, the *a* comes before another vowel, but the word does not make /a/ long a sound. This will happen throughout instruction, and it's best to stop and explain that English has exceptions to its many rules.

It is important that early childhood teachers help students understand that in English there are many words that sound the same but have different meanings, and there are words that are spelled the same and are pronounced differently and have different meanings. This is one aspect of the English language that makes it difficult, especially for ELLs.

Homophones – words that are pronounced the same but differ in meaning. A homophone may also differ in spelling.

- Here and hear
- Cell and sell
- Flour and flower

Homonyms – words that have identical spelling and pronunciation but have different meanings.

- Bark – the outside covering of a tree and the sound a dog makes
- Mean – the average and not being very nice
- Ring – a band on a finger and the sound a telephone makes
- Tire – to become fatigued and a part of a car wheel

Sight words are high frequency words that students must have automatic knowledge of. Students should memorize sight words; this helps them save their cognitive endurance for more difficult reading tasks.

- want
- what
- why
- walk
- talk
- not
- saw
- say

- said
- see
- there
- those
- been
- because
- ever
- every

- by
- are
- would
- should
- water
- called
- over
- only

Morphology

As mentioned in the previous section, when students decode, they use pieces of a word to sound out the word and figure out the meaning of the word. This is often referred to as **morphology**. The following list provides categories and examples of using morphology to develop decoding skills.

Compound words – two words put together.

Example: *mailman, sidewalk*

Root words – the basic part of the word. It stands alone in meaning and in English language often comes from Latin languages.

Example: In the word *unbelievable* the root word is *believe*. In the word *complex*, the root word is *plex*.

Prefixes – additions to root words that help to form a new word with another meaning from that of the root word. Prefixes are at the beginning of a word.

Example: Prefixes that indicate not: un- (unknown), dis- (disregard), im-(impossible), in- (inaccurate), mis-(misunderstand), and ir- (irrational).

Suffixes – additions to root words that form a new word with another meaning from that of the root word. Suffixes are at the end of a word. They change the part of speech (past tense, present tense) or verb tense of a word. They also indicate whether the word is plural or singular.

Example: -ed, -ing, and plural -s are all suffixes

Quick Tip

Etymology is the study of the origins of words and how they have changed over time. If students are analyzing root words and their meaning, students are using etymology.

For example, if students are discussing how the word *complexity* comes from the Latin word *complexus* "surrounding, encompassing," they are using etymology.

Processes and skills of word recognition

Students use a variety of processes and skills to decode words including cuing systems and morphology.

Cognitive cueing systems

As students begin to read, they use different methods to decode words. These are referred to as cueing systems. There are 3 main types of cues students use when they are in the emergent stages of reading.

1. **Semantic cues (meaning)**

   Semantic cues refer to the meaning in language that assists in comprehending texts including words, speech, signs, symbols, and other meaning-bearing forms. Semantic cues involve the learners' prior knowledge of language. Gradually, students independently relate new information to what is known and personally meaningful.

   Example: We were so hungry we had a picnic in the park.

   Picnic is a strange word, but the student can use the words *hungry* and *park* to figure out the word *picnic*.

2. **Syntactic cues (structure/grammar)**

   Syntactic cues involve the structure of the word as in the rules and patterns of language (grammar), and punctuation. As students read, they use structural cues.

   Example: The student reads, *Joey **sit** in class yesterday*.

   In this case, the student mistakes the word *sit* for *sat*. Using syntactic cuing, the student will self-correct because the word *yesterday* indicates there needs to be a past-tense verb—*sat*.

3. **Graphophonic cues (spelling)**

   Graphophonic cues involve the letter-sound or sound-symbol relationships of language. Readers identifying unknown words by relating speech sounds to letters or letter patterns are using graphophonic cues. This process is often called decoding.

   Example: The student knows that the word *make* has a long *a* sound because of the vowel after the *k*. This is a consonant, vowel, consonant, e (CVCe) word.

2. The role of fluency in literacy development

Fluency is defined as the ability to read with speed, accuracy, and proper expression, and it is a necessary skill for reading comprehension. For students to understand text, they must first read through the text fluently, so they can focus on meaning rather than sounding out words.

Comprehension is the essence of reading. This is when students begin to form images in their minds as they read. They are able to predict what might happen next in a story because they understand what is happening in the story. Students who are in the comprehension stage of reading do not need to decode (sound out) words. They read **fluently** with **prosody**, **automaticity**, and **accuracy**.

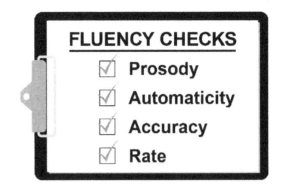

FLUENCY CHECKS
- ☑ **Prosody**
- ☑ **Automaticity**
- ☑ **Accuracy**
- ☑ **Rate**

Teachers perform fluency checks or fluency reads to measure students' reading progress. These are also called running records. While the student reads, the teacher follows along. As the student reads, the teacher checks for **automaticity**, which is effortless, speedy word recognition. The teacher also checks the student's **accuracy** and **rate**.

- **Prosody** comprises timing, phrasing, emphasis, and intonation that readers use to help convey aspects of meaning and to make their speech lively. Prosody includes stopping at periods, pausing at commas, reading with inflection, and reading with expression.

- **Automaticity** is the fast, effortless word recognition that comes with repeated reading practice. When students are reading at > 95% accuracy, they have automaticity.

- **Accuracy** is the amount of words a student reads correctly. Typically, accuracy is measured by having students read aloud during a fluency read (also called a running record). The student reads and the teacher marks any words the student miscues.

- **Rate** is the speed at which students read words correctly. Rate is typically expressed in correct words per min (wpm).

Fluency and cognitive endurance

Fluency supports cognitive endurance. When students have cognitive endurance, they read through large sections of text and build meaning from that text. Students are not wasting cognitive energy on decoding words. Instead, students are reading fluently, using their cognitive energy towards comprehension and critical thinking.

According to Lyon and Moats (1997), a young reader has only so much attentional capacity and cognitive energy to devote to a particular task. If the reading of the words on the page is slow and labored, readers simply cannot remember what they have read, much less relate the ideas they have read about to their own background knowledge. Fluent readers use less cognitive energy and are able to spend more time developing comprehension on the reading, rather than decoding words. Meaning and understanding of words can be lost in the decoding phase. That is why building automaticity and cognitive endurance is essential in developing comprehension.

Think about it!

Cognitive endurance allows students to perform tasks such as learning, reasoning, understanding, remembering, and paying attention. Building cognitive endurance allows readers to use stored cognitive energy for tasks like comprehension. If students are struggling to decode words, they are using more cognitive energy to decode and less to comprehend.

Remember: Independent reading means a student is reading at >95% accuracy.

C – Reading: Literature and Informational Text

1. Key Ideas and details

2. Text features

3. Point of view

4. Multimedia and digital literacy

5. The role of text complexity in reading development

1. Key Ideas and details

Essential comprehension skills include the ability to analyze the main ideas, supporting details and facts, author's purpose, and point of view in a piece of text. Students must also use their higher-order thinking skills to make inferences and conclusions about text.

- **Central idea.** The student can identify the story's overarching viewpoint or idea and then supports that idea with details throughout the text.

- **Supporting details and facts.** The student can identify words or phrases that help the reader answer questions about the text. The student evaluates key details by asking questions like who, what, where, when, and why.

- **Author's purpose.** The student can evaluate why the author would write the story (e.g. to inform, persuade, or describe).

- **Inference.** The student can reach a conclusion on the basis of evidence and reasoning.

- **Conclusion.** The ending of a story or essay that summarizes the overall meaning or purpose of the text.

- **Point of view.** The student can understand the perspective through which the story is told.

Quick Tip

Teachers must show students how to use evidence from the text to support students' claims. In the early childhood grades this is often done by simply asking, "Where in the story does it say that?" or, "Can you point to the place in the text that supports that?"

Characters are who the story is about. The characters in the story can be humans, animals, or even fictional creatures depending on the type of text. Understanding the characters will help with determining important components of the story.

Setting refers to the place and time the story is taking place.

Sequencing is understanding how a series of events occur in a specific and logical order. This is an important concept for students to develop because it allows students to recognize patterns that make the text and the world understandable and predictable.

Beginning   Middle   End

Plot structure allows readers and writers to visualize the key features of stories that help the student unfold important parts of the story.

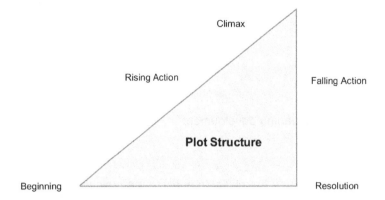

2. Text features

Using a balanced literary approach is key when teaching students how to read. A balanced literacy program uses a combination of informational and literary texts.

Informational texts are written primarily to inform and include:

- Current events
- Literary non-fiction
- Historical/social science texts
- Technical texts

Literary texts are written primarily to entertain and include:

- Adventure
- Folklore
- Fables
- Fantast

A balanced literacy program also means using a variety of genres and subgenres in classroom instruction. Effective teachers choose appropriate texts for certain occasions. Understanding genres and subgenres in both literary and informational texts will help you identify correct answers on the exam. The following table outlines the most common genres and subgenres used in an elementary reading classroom.

Test Tip

Be on the lookout for answers that include both literary and informational texts. Keep the term balanced literacy program in mind throughout the Praxis Early Childhood Test.

Genre	Subgenre
Fiction	**Realistic fiction.** Fictional stories that could be true. **Historical fiction.** Fictional stories set during a real event or time in history. These stories will have historically accurate events and locations. **Science fiction.** Fictional stories that focus on space, the future, aliens, and other galaxies. **Fantasy.** Fictional stories that include monsters, fairies, magic, and/or other fantasy elements.
Nonfiction	**Informational text.** Text that informs the reader, such as a social science textbook or informational brochure. **Biographies.** Text that tells the life of another person. The author is not the person in the biography. **Autobiographies.** Text that describes one's own life. The author is the person in the autobiography. **Expository nonfiction.** Text that informs the reader. The author is objective. **Narrative nonfiction.** Text that presents a true story written in a style more closely associated with fiction.
Poetry	**Limerick.** A humorous verse of three long and two short lines rhyming (AABBA). **Sonnet.** A poem of 14 lines using any of a number of formal rhyme schemes. **Epic.** A long narrative that focuses on the trials and tribulations of a hero or god-like character who represents the cultural values of a race, nation, or religious group. **Haiku.** A Japanese poem consisting of 3 lines and 17 syllables. Each line has a set number of syllables: line 1 has 5 syllables; line 2 has 7 syllables; line 3 has 5 syllables.
Folklore	**Fable.** A short story that includes animals who speak and act like humans. There is usually a moral at the end of a fable. **Myth.** A story that showcases gods or goddesses and typically outlines the creation of something. **Legend.** A story that may have once been true but is exaggerated, usually about extraordinary human beings. **Fairy tale.** A story that has both human and magical creatures in it.
Dramas	**Comedy.** Entertainment consisting of jokes and satirical sketches intended to make an audience laugh. **Tragedy.** A play dealing with tragic events and having an unhappy ending, especially concerning the downfall of the main character.

As students begin to navigate informational text like textbooks, and complex information, teachers can also show students how to use text features to locate information.

Text Feature	Description	Example
Heading	Bold words or phrases that separate the text by main ideas.	**Reptiles in the Wild** Reptiles are cold-blooded—they rely on heat from their surroundings to stay warm or to stay cool. Reptiles have lungs. Most species of reptiles eat other animals and lay eggs on land to breed.
Glossary	Used to find the meanings of important words in the text.	**Cold-blooded** - Having a body temperature varying with that of the environment; poikilothermic. **Reptile** - A vertebrate animal of a class that includes snakes, lizards, crocodiles, turtles, and tortoises. They are distinguished by having dry, scaly skin and typically laying soft-shelled eggs on land.
Index	Used to reference certain aspects of the text using page numbers where those ideas are found. An index is in alphabetical order.	**R** Rattlesnakes 23 Reptiles in the Wild 34 Respiratory Systems 15 Reproduction 44
Graphs/ Charts	Representation of data in visual form.	Diet of a Reptile (bar chart with values 0–5 on vertical axis; categories A, B, C on horizontal axis; legend: A, B, C)

Text Feature	Description	Example
Sidebar	More information found on the side or bottom of a website.	**Menu Tab** Sidebar information / Content Footer information
Hyperlink	Used to point the reader to additional information. Brings the reader to another website or file and is usually indicated with a different color text that is underlined.	www.Reptiles.com/american-aligator

Understanding structural elements of text can positively impact students' literacy skills. When students understand the structure of text, they can construct, examine, and extend the meaning in text, which leads to a depth of understand of the text.

Text structure refers to how the information is organized in the text and can help students identify the following elements of the text.

- **Main idea and details.** The story or passage has an overarching theme or idea and details throughout the text that support for that idea.

- **Compare and contrast.** The story or text highlights similarities and differences between and among people, places, and situations.

- **Chronological.** The story or passage is sequential or follows an order or timeline.

- **Cause and effect.** The story or passage presents something that happens and then the result or effect of an action.

- **Problem and solution.** The story or passage presents a problem and then possible solutions to the problem.

- **Inferences.** The reader draws a conclusion based on evidence and reasoning. The reader can make a logical "guess" based on something that is happening in the story.

- **Key details.** The reader uses words or phrases in the story or passage to answer questions about the text. Key details give information by asking questions like who, what, where, when, and why.

3. Point of view

Essential comprehension skills include the ability to analyze the main ideas, supporting details and facts, author's purpose, and point of view in a piece of text. Students must also use their higher-order thinking skills to make inferences and conclusions about text.

Point of View	Definition
First person	A narrator in the story recounts his or her own perspective, experience or impressions. The pronouns *I*, *we*, *me*, *us*, are used in the text.
Second person	The story is written in the perspective of *you*.
Third person objective	The narrator remains a detached observer, telling only the story's action and dialogue
Third person limited	The narrator tells the story from the viewpoint of one character in the story.
Third person omniscient	The narrator has unlimited knowledge and can describe every character's thoughts and interpret every character's behavior. Omniscient means all-knowing.

Quick Tip

Third person narrative is often used in informational text because it is the most objective point of view.

4. Multimedia and digital literacy

Students comprehend text in a variety of ways. The following practices outline how to integrate different types of text and how they are useful to students who are learning to read.

Audio books are used to help students follow along in a book as a narrator reads aloud. This is often done in centers. This practice is extremely helpful for students because they hear the reader's fluency and prosody, which helps with students' reading skills.

Basal reading books are leveled text students can use at the beginning of their reading acquisition. The old-fashioned Dick and Jane books are basal readers.

Graphic novels use visual illustrations to portray a story and require students to use inference skills to understand the meaning of the text.

Picture books help students with semantic cueing and aid in comprehension. Picture books are essential tools in helping students with their early reading.

5. The role of text complexity in reading development

Text complexity

When developing a balanced literacy approach in the classroom, teachers must use several data points to measure text complexity. It is important for teachers to select appropriate text levels because classrooms consist of students with varying abilities.

Measures of Text Complexity	
Qualitative	This type of data *cannot* be quantified. Instead, this data often comes in the form of anecdotal responses or scenarios. **Example**: While a teacher is observing students as they read, she notices some students are struggling. She decides to intervene with a different text or targeted interventions.
Quantitative	Data that *can* be quantified. When analyzing this type of data, teachers often look over reading levels, words per min and other measures that can be represented as numbers. **Example**: A teacher uses students' correct words per minute to determine the Lexile levels of books they will use in the next lesson.
Reader and task	These are the reader variables (motivation, knowledge, and experience) and task variables (purpose and complexity generated by the task assigned and the question posed). These variables can be measured both qualitatively and quantitatively. **Example**: A teacher chooses books that students have expressed interest in. The teacher understands the students are more likely to engage in text they are motivated to read.

This page intentionally left blank.

D – Writing

1. The developmental stages of writing
2. Characteristics of common types of writing
3. The writing process
4. Characteristics of effective writing
5. Digital media literacy for text production
6. The research process

1. The developmental stages of writing

Writing at the developmental stage means that children begin to understand that writing is a form of communication and their marks on paper convey a message (Mayer, 2007).

- **Preliterate drawing.** The student uses drawing to stand for writing and believes that the drawings/writing are communicating a purposeful message.

- **Preliterate scribbling.** The student scribbles but intends the scribbles to be writing. The scribbling resembles writing. During this stage, the student holds the pencil correctly.

- **Emergent.** The student uses random letters or drawings. Students at this stage also use letter sequences and may write long strings of numbers in random order.

- **Transitional.** The student continues to use a variety of different strategies to spell more difficult words. Students at this stage often use inventive spelling

Preliterate to Emergent	
Scribbling	Random marks or scribbles often occur on a page with drawings. Children may say, "This says Tommy!" (child's name).
Emergent	
Mock handwriting or wavy scribble	Children produce lines of wavy scribbles as they imitate adult cursive writing. Children will often pretend they are writing something they have seen their parents write such as a grocery list or a letter.
Mock letters	Children attempt to form alphabetic representations, which also often appear in their drawings. Writing in this stage is often vertical versus horizontal. Children make shapes that resemble conventional letters.

Transitional	
Conventional letters	Children begin to write letters, usually from their name or a family member's name. As children's mock letters become more and more conventional, real letters of the alphabet begin to appear. Children will often create strings of letters across a page and "read" them as real sentences or a series of sentences.
Invented spelling (also known as approximated or phonetic spelling)	Children write words using phonemic awareness. The words are not spelled correctly but do resemble the sounds of the words. For example, invented spelling of the word *was* may be *wuz*, or the invented spelling of the word *other* may be *uther*.
Fluent	
Conventional spellings	Children's approximated spellings gradually become more and more conventional. The child's own name is usually written first, followed by words such as *mom*, *dad*, and *love*. Initially, children may incorrectly copy words. Eventually, words will be written correctly. Adults can support the child's move to conventional spelling by being patient and by continuing to serve as a good writing model.

2. Characteristics of common types of writing

Modes of writing

There are four modes of writing:

1. **Opinion/argumentative.** Writing that persuades or convinces using support, details, and examples from the text in logical order. In early grades, this is called *opinion writing*.

2. **Informative/explanatory.** Writing that informs, explains, or tells "how to" without using opinions (just the facts).

3. **Descriptive.** Writing that describes or helps form a visual picture using sensory details and spatial order.

4. **Narrative.** A first-person account that tells a story as it happens using sensory details and chronological order.

Point of view impacts the relationship the reader has with the story. The world the author is attempting to create depends on the point of view.

Point of view	Definition	Example
1st person	The story is told from a character in the story *Key words: I, me, she*	*Tales of the fourth Grade Nothing* by Judy Blume
2nd person	Puts the reading in the story *Key words: you, your*	Recipe books, instructions, how-to books, choose your own adventure books
3rd person	The narrator is not in the story. *Key words: she/he, her/his*	*Where the Red Fern Grows* by Wilson Rawls

Students can use the different types of text structures to organize their writing. The following table outlines the types of text structures used in writing.

Text Structure	Definition	Example
Compare and contrast	Analyzes two or more items to establish similarities/ differences.	*The hungry bunny eats grass, while the hungry hawk eats rabbits.*
Chronological sequence	Gives information in order of occurrence.	*First, settlers arrived in the colonies and built their homes. Next, settlers began to farm. Finally, settlers set up a government.*
Spatial sequence	Describes things as they appear.	*The store was located just south of the old bridge and to the east of Dr. Miller's office.*
Cause and effect	Gives reason/explanation for happening.	*One of the reasons grasses are producers is because grasses are considered plants that make their own food. This allows grasses to produce energy in the form of carbohydrates for animals to eat.*
Problem and solution	Sets up a problem and outlines a solution.	*The third pig knew the wolf would be coming to the neighborhood, so he built his house out of strong brick.*
Description	Descriptive details about characteristics, actions, etc.	*The traveler came upon a beautiful meadow with vibrant green grass and a cloudless sky.*

3. The writing process

Effective writing teachers guide students through the stages of writing and authoring process.

Authoring process

1. **Pre-writing.** Brainstorming, considering purpose and goals for writing, using graphic organizers to connect ideas, and designing a coherent structure for a writing piece.

2. **Drafting.** Working independently to draft the sentence, essay, or paper.

3. **Peer review.** Students evaluate each other's writing for content and understanding.

4. **Revising.** Reworking a piece of writing based on structure, tone, and clear connections.

5. **Editing.** Editing based on conventions and mechanics.

6. **Rewriting.** Incorporating changes as they carefully write or type their final drafts.

7. **Publishing.** Producing and disseminating the work in a variety of ways, such as a class book, bulletin board, letters to the editor, school newsletter, or website.

Test Tip

When answering questions on the Praxis Early Childhood test, look for answer choices where the teacher focuses on the revision process in writing. Writing teachers must emphasize that effective writing only happens after many edits and revisions.

4. Characteristics of effective writing

Writing clearly and coherently is extremely challenging for elementary-age students. Therefore, teachers must provide students with tools to help with the writing process. There are several ways teachers can help students write clearly and coherently.

- **Organization.** It is important that students organize their writing by first mapping what they are going to write. Mind maps and other graphic organizers can help students do this.

- **Transitional words.** These words connect parts of a paragraph to one another. Helping students identify the right transitional words is useful in coherent writing.

- **Cooperative learning.** These writing workshops help students revise their writing. Peer reviews, brainstorming sessions, and editing roundtables can help students revise their writing in an effective manner. It is important to remember that for cooperative learning to be effective, it must be organized, and everyone in the group must have a role.

- **Frameworks.** These formulas allow students to follow a step-by-step structure as they write. This allows students to plug their information into the pre-established formula. As the students get more proficient in writing, they can modify or abandon the formula.

- **Rubrics.** These assessment tools outline expectations for student writing. Students should not have to guess what the teacher wants to see in the writing assignment. Rubrics outline a set of parameters that help students focus their writing.

On the exam, you may be required to identify effective instructional methods for teaching writer's craft. Writer's craft is the techniques, language, and approaches used in writing to make the writing appealing to the reader. Writer's craft includes using:

Linking words (transition words). These are words that link two ideas and are used to provide sentence variety in writing. Linking words include:

- For example,
- In addition,
- However,
- Therefore,

Precise language. Language that clarifies or identifies specific details. When students use precise language, they are using details that allow the reader or listener to understand the story.

Figurative language. Using metaphor, imagery, hyperbole, etc. in writing to make the writing interesting. Examples include:

- She was as thirsty as a camel in the desert.
- The sun was an orange in the sky.

Temporal words (time). These are used to indicate time. These words include:

- Meanwhile
- At that moment
- Before
- After
- Then
- Next

Dialogue. These words are used to show a conversation or verbal exchange between characters.

- The woman ran into the room shouting, "They've robbed the bank!"

Sentence variety. Refers to the practice of varying the length and structure of sentences to avoid monotony and provide appropriate emphasis. It makes the writing lively and unpredictable. It is pleasing to the reader. Using transition words, punctuation, and complex sentences all contribute to sentence variety.

- These sentences lack variety: *He went to the store. He bought a candy bar. He was happy.*

- This sentence has variety: *He went to the story and bought a candy bar, which made him happy.*

Example question

Use the student sample below to answer the following question.

Julie and Mary go to the same school. July likes math. Mary likes reading class. Julie and Mary have been friends for a long time.

Which of the following activities can the teacher use to help this student with his writing?

   A. Use a linking words activity to help the student achieve sentence variety in his writing.

   B. Work on a punctuation worksheet to improve the students use of periods.

   C. Diagram sentence to help the student understand prepositional phrases.

   D. Work on modes of writing so the student can improve persuasive writing.

Correct answer: A

This writing lacks transitional words or linking words to achieve sentence variety. As is, the sentences are robotic. Therefore, answer A is the best choice.

Writing conventions

On the exam, you might be asked to identify errors in student writing. You might also be asked to provide appropriate feedback on student writing. The questions will contain basic grammar errors. Below is a list of grammar expectations for elementary students.

- **Parts of speech**. Noun, verb, adjective, adverb

- **Fragments**. Non-sentences, phrases that do not have a subject and a predicate

- **Subject verb agreement**. The subject and the predicate must agree. For example, *the girl **run** to the car* should be *the **girl runs** to the car*.

Rubrics

Rubrics are used to convey expectations and criteria of an assessment. Rubrics are often used to grade students' writing. Rubrics provide an explicit breakdown of the elements assessed. Rubrics also provide teachers with a framework to implement specific and meaningful feedback.

Rubrics should be given to students:

- **Before** writing to convey explicit expectations.

- **During** writing so students can check their progress.

- **After** writing to communicate grades/progress.

Example Rubric

	1 - Minimal	2 - Meets	3 - Exceeds
Mechanics (Syntactic)	Many spelling, grammar, and punctuation errors; sentence fragments; incorrect use of capitalization.	Some spelling and grammar errors; most sentences have punctuation and are complete; uses uppercase and lowercase letters.	Correct spelling, grammar, and punctuation; complete sentences; correct use of capitalization.
Ideas and Content (Semantic)	Key words are not near the beginning; no clear topic; no beginning, middle, and end; ideas are not ordered.	Main idea or topic is in first sentence; semi-defined topic; attempts beginning, middle and end sections; some order of main idea and details in sequence.	Interesting, well-stated main idea or topic sentence; uses logical plan with an effective beginning, middle, and end; good flow of ideas from topic sentence to details in sequence.
Organization	Very unorganized and confusing.	Organized enough to read and understand the ideas.	Very organized and easy to understand.

Quick Tip

Feedback on student writing should be specific and meaningful. This can be done with detailed comments on the paper. One-to-on conferences about their writing is most effective. Whatever feedback a teacher gives, it should be framed in a positive manner with specific elements students can work on. For example, "You did a great job with your complex sentences. Now let's try to use proper punctuation here and here to make it grammatically correct."

5. Digital media literacy for text production

Media literacy is the ability to think critically about information from newspapers, websites, blogs, and social networks in order to determine the information's validity.

Considerations when using media literacy:

- Is this fact or opinion?
- What type of media is being used?
- Who is conveying the message and why?

Technology should enhance the learning experience. Teachers have the opportunity to use a variety of different technologies in the classroom. Whatever technology teachers choose, it should be age-appropriate, meaning it should not be too complex for young learners or too easy for advanced learners. Technology should also reflect the task students are being asked to perform.

Textbooks vs. Computers

Textbook Pros	Computer Pros
Students are able to use something tangible. No matter how amazing technology gets, students still love physical books.	The computer can increase the question complexity when a student begins to answer questions correctly.
Students can read text in physical books more easily than they can read on computers.	The computer can store a large number of textbooks in its memory.

6. The research process

Students start to use the Internet and other resources at a young age to find and sort information. Early in their academic careers, students are expected to conduct research. It is the job of the teacher to guide students in finding reliable, relevant, and scholarly research.

Steps to the research process

There is not a definitive set of steps for the research process. However, most models follow a similar structure. Teaching young children this process will help them as they progress through school and into college and career. Here is the basic framework of the research process.

1. Choose a topic.
2. Generate a few questions about that topic—who, what, when, where, how.
3. Find information the topic by using digital tools like the Internet or traditional publications like books.
4. Refine the topic—go from general to specific.
5. Take notes and summarize information.
6. Organize information.
7. Share the research in a presentation, paper, discussion, etc.

Research methods

Students will use a variety of primary and secondary resources when they write research papers. It is important that teachers help students identify relevant primary and secondary resources and cite them appropriately.

	Humanities	Sciences
Primary sources (original source)	• Diaries, journals, letters • Interviews with people who lived during a particular time (e.g., survivors of genocide in Rwanda or the Holocaust) • Songs, plays, novels, stories • Paintings, drawings, sculptures • Autobiographies	• Published results of research studies • Published results of scientific experiments • Published results of clinical trials • Proceedings of conferences and meetings

	Humanities	Sciences
Secondary sources (interpretation of the original source)	• Biographies • Histories • Literary criticism • Book, art, theater reviews • Newspaper articles that interpret	• Publications about the significance of research or experiments • Analysis of a clinical trial • Review of the results of several experiments or trials

Evaluating sources

It is important to evaluate source information for relevancy. This is especially important when using Internet sources. Understanding credibility in resources is essential for scoring well on the exam.

Sources	Definition	Examples
Reliable sources	A trustworthy source of information.	• Published results of research studies • Published results of scientific experiments • Published results of clinical trials • Proceedings of conferences and meetings
Unreliable sources	An unqualified and unreliable source to support ideas.	• Online blogs about a particular topic • Chats or discussion forums on the Internet • Websites from private companies

Avoiding plagiarism

It is imperative that students learn from a young age how to paraphrase information into their own words. Teachers can help students do this by showing students how to take notes that summarize a topic or idea. Teachers can also encourage students to cite information when the student has taken an idea or excerpt from a text.

Paraphrasing. Restating a text, passage, or work to express the meaning in another form (Merriam-Webster Dictionary, 2019).

Plagiarizing. Passing off the ideas or words of another as one's own; using another's work without crediting the source (Merriam-Webster Dictionary, 2019).

IMPORTANT: Even if a student paraphrases content, if the idea or information was obtained from someone else's work, it MUST be cited in the text.

E – Speaking and Listening

1. Characteristics of effective collaborative conversations
2. Characteristics of engaging oral presentations

1. Characteristics of effective collaborative conversations

There are several instructional methods teachers can use to develop speaking and listening skills. First collaborative conversations and discussions are effective ways to foster communication skills. In these activities, students apply their knowledge and skills by actively engaging in conversation with peers.

When students are beginning to read, visual and oral enhanced books can help them move through the text and derive meaning. In addition, using multimedia to explain text or allowing students to use multimedia to represent their understanding of the text, can increase comprehension of text. This can help students as they communicate about the text.

Collaborative conversations and discussions. These typically occur in literature circles or workshop situations. In these activities, students debate topics, identify problems and solutions, and use their experiences to communicate with one another.

Multimedia presentation. These include information presented with slides, video, or digital representations.

Modeling. One way to help students in their abilities to be active listeners and to participate in collaborative discussions is to model that behavior. This can be done through metacognition techniques where the teacher models the thinking process and how to use their brains to be active listeners.

Effective language arts and reading teachers focus part of their instruction on speaking and listening. These skills are essential in the reading process. Teachers do this by showing students how to be active listeners.

Steps in the active listening process are as follows:

- Look at the person. Put everything else away and pay attention to the speaker.
- Listen to the words and understand how the speaker is feeling.
- Be interested in what the person is talking about.
- Restate what is being said.
- Ask questions for clarification.
- Be aware of your own opinions and feelings on the subject.
- Restate what the speaker has said. For example, "I hear you when you say, 'I am feeling frustrated with this assignment.'"

Appropriate feedback for active listening can be done verbally and nonverbally.

Verbal Signals	Non-Verbal Signals
• "I'm listening" • Disclosures • Statements of validation • Support statements • Reflecting/mirroring statements	• Appropriate eye contact (when culturally appropriate) • Facial expressions • Body language • Silence • Touching (when culturally appropriate)

2. Characteristics of engaging oral presentations

When teaching students to engage in oral presentations, teachers should focus on certain principles. Teaching these skills can help students understand how to successfully give presentations that are clear and coherent. Using the Common Core State Standards to review grade-level expectations will help with using the characteristics appropriately in different grade levels.

Characteristic	Explanation
Volume	Using appropriate volume to deliver a clear presentation.
Articulation	Articulation is defined as the movement of the tongue, lips, and jaw in order to make the specific speech sounds.
Awareness of Audience	Understanding what the audience needs and delivering that information as effectively as possible.

It is important that students understand that effective and engaging presentations

- Have clear objectives
- Are useful to the audience
- Are practiced or rehearsed
- Contain visuals and other helpful tools
- Include audience participation in some form

Early childhood teachers must demonstrate the difference between formal and informal language and when to use formal and informal language.

Test Tip

Oral presentations are a part of teaching students speaking and listening skills. Oral presentations involve volume, articulation, and audience awareness. For the exam, remember those three aspects of oral presentations.

- **Colloquialisms** are informal words and phrases. Another way to refer to colloquial language is *slang*. Colloquialisms are greatly affected by social influences.

- **Denotative meaning** is the dictionary meaning of a word. For example, the denotative meaning of *cool* is cold, or at a low temperature.

- **Connotative meaning** is the implied meaning. For example, the connotative meaning of the word *cool* is easy going, popular, or stylish.

Being a respectful audience member

Equally important as being an effective presenter, students must learn how to be respectful audience members when their peers are presenting. This is done a number of ways.

- Pay attention
- Listen actively
- Ask relevant questions

F – Language

1. Conventions of standard English grammar, usage, mechanics, and spelling
2. Vocabulary instruction
3. Conversational, academic, and domain-specific language

1. Conventions of standard English grammar, usage, mechanics, and spelling

Beginning at an early age, students will be able to identify parts of speech. There are 8 parts of speech listed in the table below.

Part of Speech	Definition	Example
Noun	Person, place or thing.	**Stan** has a new **bike**.
Verb	Action or state of being.	Judy **ran** towards the ball.
Adjective	Describes nouns or pronouns.	Sam showed off his **silver** coin.
Adverb	Modifies verbs, adjectives, and adverbs.	He ran **quickly** across the street.
Preposition	Shows relationships of nouns or pronouns to other words.	I left the book **on** the table.
Pronoun	Replaces a noun.	**She** was the only one at the party without a gift.
Conjunction	Joins to phrases together.	She was happy **but** also nervous.
Injection	Expresses strong emotion.	**Hey**! I haven't seen you in a long time!

Language conventions are the accepted use or practice of spelling and punctuation.

Orthography

Orthography refers to conventional spelling and the rules associated with spelling. Remember, there are exceptions to these rules.

- Use *i* before *e*, except after *c*, or when sounding like *a* as *neighbor* and *weight*.
- Drop the final *e* when adding a suffix that starts with a vowel, but not when adding a suffix starting with a consonant.
- Change the final *y* to *i* before adding a suffix unless the suffix begins with *i*.
- Double a final single consonant before adding a suffix when the word ends with a single vowel followed by a single consonant and when the consonant ends an accented syllable or a one-syllable word.
- The letter *q* is typically followed by the letter *u*.
- To change a word that ends with a *y* to be plural, change the *y* to *i* and add *es*.

Standard spelling conventions

There are an infinite number of spelling patterns that could be presented on the exam. Spelling is sometimes assessed by using commonly confused words.

Sentence Structure

Effective writers use a mix of compound and complex sentences to illustrate sentence variety, which adds vibrancy and interest to text. You will see questions on the exam about helping students increase their writing skills by using sentence variety.

Quick Tip

Spelling patterns

Students will use hard consonant sounds first when spelling words. For example, if students are in the early stages of the spelling continuum, they might spell the word *flowers* as *FLRS*. They may spell the word *sun* as *SN*. The next step would be to introduce medial vowel sounds so they can begin to see where vowels fit into the words.

Sentence Type	Explanation	Example
Simple sentence	Consists of one **independent** clause	I went to the store.
Compound sentence	Consists of **two independent** clauses. Ensure that there is a comma between two independent clauses in a compound sentence. The comma should be followed by a coordinating conjunction (**FANBOYS**)	I went to the store, and I bought milk.
Complex sentence	Consists of an independent clause and a dependent clause. When the sentence starts with a dependent clause, a comma is needed after the clause.	When I went to the store, I bought milk.
Compound complex sentence	Consists of at least two independent clauses, and at least one dependent clause.	When I went to the store, I bought milk, and I bought cheese.

Identifying independent and dependent clauses

The best approach to this part of the assessment is to understand the difference between independent clauses and dependent clauses.

- An **independent clause** contains a subject and a verb and expresses a complete thought. An independent clause can stand on its own as a sentence.

- A **dependent clause** contains a noun and a verb but does not express a complete thought. A dependent clause cannot be a sentence on its own.

Example:

Dependent Clause

While we waited for the bus, we discussed the details of our presentation.

Independent Clause

Fragments

Dependent clauses, without the independent clause in a sentence, are fragments. Fragments are not sentences.

Incorrect:

Independent Clause

She often wears a helmet when she rides her bike. **Worrying she will fall and hurt herself.**

Dependent Clause

Correct:

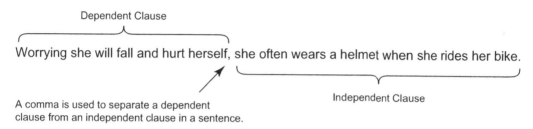

Dependent Clause

Worrying she will fall and hurt herself, she often wears a helmet when she rides her bike.

Independent Clause

A comma is used to separate a dependent clause from an independent clause in a sentence.

Quick Tip

You can take a fragment and add it to an independent clause to make a complete sentence as long as you place a comma, separating them appropriately.

Varieties in the English Language

When students engage with text, they will often encounter dialect and register.

Dialect refers to a variation of a language that is characteristic of the users of that language.

Register refers to a variation of a language that is determined by use—a situation or context.

Varieties of English (e.g., dialects, registers) used in stories, dramas, or poems support the overall meaning of text

Variety of English	Example
Dialect	*Huckleberry Finn* by Mark Twain Jim: "We's safe, Huck, we's safe! Jump up and crack yo' heels. Dat's de good ole Cairo at las', I jis knows it." Huck: "I'll take the canoe and go see, Jim. It mightn't be, you know."
Register	People speak differently in church than they do on the street. Also, people speak differently at work than they do with friends.

2. Vocabulary instruction

We mentioned this previously; however, it is worth mentioning it again because it fits in this category. As students begin to read, they use different methods to decode words. These are referred to as cueing systems. There are 3 main types of cues students use when they are in the emergent stages of reading.

1. **Semantic cues**

   Semantic cues refer to the meaning in language that assists in comprehending texts including words, speech, signs, symbols, and other meaning-bearing forms. Semantic cues involve the learners' prior knowledge of language. Gradually, students independently relate new information to what is known and personally meaningful.

   Example: We were so hungry we had a picnic in the park.

   Picnic is a strange word, but the student can use the words *hungry* and *park* to figure out the word *picnic*.

2. **Syntactic cues**

   Syntactic cues involve the structure of the word as in the rules and patterns of language (grammar), and punctuation. As students read, they use structural cues.

   Example: The student reads, Joey **sit** *in class yesterday*.

   In this case, the student mistakes the word *sit* for *sat*. Using syntactic cuing, the student will self-correct because the word *yesterday* indicates there needs to be a past-tense verb—*sat*.

3. **Graphophonic cues**

   Graphophonic cues involve the letter-sound or sound-symbol relationships of language. Readers identifying unknown words by relating speech sounds to letters or letter patterns are using graphophonic cues. This process is often called decoding.

Types of Figurative Language

Identifying types of figurative language is also a way to determine meaning in text. Students will encounter lots of figurative language in stories, fables, poems, and informational text.

Device	Definition	Examples
Simile	Using *like* or *as*.	She was as thin as a rail.
Imagery	A description that conveys a clear picture to the reader.	The big, juicy burger with its melted cheese and ripe tomatoes made my mouth water.
Metaphor	Applying word or phrase to an individual or thing without using the word *like* or *as*.	He was a lion filled with rage.
Personification	Attributing human characteristics to something not human.	The cat judged me from across the room.
Onomatopoeia	The formation of a word from a sound associated with it.	Sizzle, kurplunk, POW!, BAM!

Device	Definition	Examples
Hyperbole	Exaggerated statements or claims not meant to be taken literally.	The cake must have weighed 500 pounds!
Idioms	A word or phrase that means something different from its literal meaning.	It's raining cats and dogs.
Alliteration	When words that start with the same sound are used repeatedly in a phrase or sentence.	Wearing pink pants, Paul picked purple pickles.
Irony	Expression of one's meaning by using language that normally signifies the opposite, typically for humorous or emphatic effect.	It was raining on National Picnic Day.
Foreshadow	When the author uses clues or imagery to express what might happen next.	The dark spot on the ceiling grew bigger and bigger. This is written before a pipe bursts and floods the house.

3. Conversational, academic, and domain-specific language

There are a variety of ways to approach vocabulary instruction. Teaching vocabulary in context is essential. However, students must also use definitions and parts of speech to figure out words. Just like all instruction, vocabulary instruction should be differentiated to meet the specific needs of every student. The following are the findings of the National Reading Panel's research. You will find scenarios with these types of approaches in the correct answers on the language and literacy section of the exam.

Best Practices for Vocabulary Instruction

- Intentional instruction of vocabulary items is required for specific texts.

- Repetition and multiple exposures to vocabulary items are important.

- Learning in rich contexts is valuable for vocabulary learning. Vocabulary tasks should be restructured as necessary.

- Vocabulary learning should entail active engagement in learning tasks.

- Computer technology can be used effectively to help teach vocabulary.

- Vocabulary can be acquired through incidental learning. How vocabulary is assessed and evaluated can have differential effects on instruction.

- Dependence on a single vocabulary instructional method will not result in optimal learning.

Quick Tip

Learning vocabulary in context is also referred to as **incidental vocabulary**. Incidental vocabulary learning is the unintended learning of words that occurs in the course of engagement in other activities. This is the real-world application of vocabulary and is regarded by some scholars as the most effective form of word learning.

The following table provides some dos and don'ts to be on the lookout for when taking your exam.

Do	Don't
Have students use context to figure out difficult words.	Have students write words over and over again.
Use interactive word walls so students can engage with new vocabulary.	Have students copy definitions from the glossary.
Model think aloud strategies for students to use when faced with difficult academic and domain specific words.	Assign extra vocabulary homework for those who struggle.

Vocabulary differs from content area to content area. For example, the words used in science class can be much different than the words used history class. Those words are different than words used in general conversation. Teachers must prepare students to engage with conversation, general academic, and domain specific words. Vocabulary words are usually organized as tier I, II, or III words.

Caution

Avoid answer choices that describe memorizing vocabulary words or copying down definitions of vocabulary words. These practices are usually the wrong answer on the test.

Language and Literacy Practice Questions

1. A teacher reads the story *The Giving Tree* to 1st grade students. She has students use a graphic organizer where they match pictures from the story to the beginning, middle, and end. The students then share their graphic organizers with a partner. Which of the following concepts of literary structure is the class working on?

   A. Character development

   B. Plot sequence

   C. Point of view

   D. Setting

2. A kindergarten teacher displays an oversized book in the front of the class. As the teacher reads the lines in the book, she sweeps her hand from left to right, indicating how students read in English. The teacher is working on what type of concept of print?

   A. Directionality

   B. Sequencing

   C. Leveling

   D. Pictures

3. A teacher has students say the word *cat*. Then she asks students to say the word *cat* without the /c/ sound. What is the class working on?

   A. Phonological awareness

   B. Phonics

   C. Semantics

   D. Phonemic awareness

4. Students are using the chart below for a classroom activity. They are matching different parts of the words to make a whole word. What are the students working on?

tr		ack
br		ake
st		ick
pl		an

   A. Onset and rime

   B. Phonemic awareness

   C. Cueing systems

   D. Syllables

5. Which of the following would be considered a CVCe word?

   A. brake

   B. make

   C. back

   D. bat

6. Students in a 3rd grade class are learning the difference between opinion and fact. Which of the following activities would be most effective in helping students understand the difference?

   A. Have a guest speaker come in and talk about bias in commercials.

   B. Have students read about fact and opinion in their cooperative groups.

   C. Display different advertisements in the front of the class and discuss why some use facts while others use opinion.

   D. Have students complete a multiple-choice test on fact vs opinion and then discuss their answers.

7. A 1st grade teacher is introducing students to effective writing. Which of the following should be the focus of students' writing?

   A. Length, time, interest

   B. Visuals, outline, brainstorm

   C. Task, audience, purpose

   D. Legibility, readability, word count

8. What is the most effective approach when helping students construct essays or short stories?

   A. Focus on legibility.

   B. Focus on vocabulary.

   C. Focus on handwriting.

   D. Focus on revision.

9. A student is reading through a piece of text. When he gets to a difficult word, he uses pictures and other words to determine the unknown word's meaning. The student is using which cueing system?

   A. Semantic

   B. Syntactic

   C. Graphophonic

   D. Pragmatic

10. Which of the following would be the most effective approach to helping students with varying needs in literacy?

   A. Lower the standards so those struggling can meet their goals.

   B. Differentiate instruction and accommodate learners in meeting their goals.

   C. Pair students with more advanced students for peer tutoring.

   D. Use incentives to motivate students to meet their goals.

Number	Answer	Explanation
1.	B	The key words here are *beginning, middle, and end*, which indicate story sequence.
2.	A	The key words here are *left* to *right,* which indicate directionality. This is a concept of print. In the United States, students read from left to right and top to bottom.
3.	D	This is a deletion activity. Because the students are only using the sounds in words with this activity, this is a phonemic awareness activity.
4.	A	This activity is an onset and rime activity. The onset is the beginning consonant and consonant cluster in a word. In this case, *tr, br, st,* and *pl* are the onsets. Rimes are the vowel and consonants that follow the onset. In this case, the rimes are *ack, ake, ick,* and *an.*
5.	B	In this case, *C* stands for consonant, and *V* stands for vowel. In this question, you are asked to find the CVCe word, which is a word that has a consonant, long vowel, consonant, then a silent *e* at the end. The word *make* is a CVCe word.
6.	C	Answer C is the best answer because students are looking at actual advertisements which brings the activity into the real world. A guest speaker, in answer A, is not effective because that is essentially a lecture on the subject. Multiple choice tests are usually not the correct answer on this exam, especially for young students.
7.	C	Always remember, when teaching students effective writing, task, audience and purpose are the most important aspects to consider.
8.	D	Revision is one of the most important aspects of writing and teachers must help students understand that good writing means making many revisions. This can be done with specific and meaningful feedback and a focus on revisions in workshops and peer reviews.
9.	A	Using the sematic cueing system has to do with the word's meaning. Syntactic is the structure of the word. Graphophonic is the spelling of the word. Finally, pragmatic is the way the word is use in a social context.
10.	B	Differentiation and accommodation are on the "good words" list. You never want to lower expectations. That is always the wrong answer. Pairing students with other students is ok, but it is really the job of the teacher to make sure students are getting what they need. Finally, giving extrinsic rewards is a practice on the "bad words" list and is usually not the correct answer on these exams.

II. Mathematics

A – Emergent Mathematics: Foundational Skills

1. Prerequisite skills needed for mathematical skills development

   - Patterns

   - One-to-one correspondence

   - Grouping and classification

   - Subitizing

   - Sequencing and conservation of numbers

   - Position and proximity

   - Multiple representations of numbers

   - Counting and cardinality principles

1. Prerequisite skills needed for mathematical skills development

Students' thinking evolves as they interact with math. Understanding math is just like understanding anything; you start with the concrete and move toward the abstract.

Think CRA!

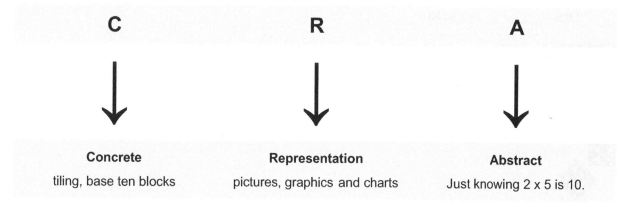

C	**R**	**A**
Concrete	**Representation**	**Abstract**
tiling, base ten blocks	pictures, graphics and charts	Just knowing 2 x 5 is 10.

Fluency in elementary mathematics relates to the speed and accuracy by which a student can answer a basic math fact. Math fact fluency is a four-step process.

- **Accuracy.** Solving problems using a correct method and arriving at the correct answer. This step relates to a student's understanding, not speed or recall.

- **Automaticity.** Exploring efficient strategies for finding the correct answer. Students achieving automaticity can give a correct answer as an automatic response.

- **Rate.** Working toward quick recall of a math fact. Students who are fluent in math facts can respond to an answer at a quick rate.

- **Flexibility.** Choosing and explaining different strategies for arriving at a correct answer. This step relates to a student's deep understanding, not speed or recall.

When teaching foundational math skills, educators must understand the prerequisite skills needed for future math skills. The following are prerequisite math skills you will see on the exam.

Recognizing patterns

It is important to recognize, analyze, and apply different methods for teaching mathematical concepts and procedures. Students must be able to understand repeated core patterns like the following:

One-to-one correspondence

One-to-one correspondence is a counting and quantity principle that refers to the understanding that each object in a group can be counted once and only once. It is useful in the early stages for children to tag or touch each item being counted and to move it out of the way as it is counted. This is usually done using manipulatives or physical objects.

Grouping and classification by one or more attributes

Students must learn to group and sort objects based on attributes. An example activity might be having students grab a handful of blue and green tiles and then fill out the sentences below.

- I have _____ blue tiles.

- I have _____ green tiles.

- I have more _____ tiles than _____ tiles.

- I have _____ tiles in all.

Subitizing

A student's ability to quickly identify a number of items in a small group without having to count them, regardless of the arrangement of items. For example, using the dice below, a student can quickly assert the number is six on both. The student does not have to count then dots to know that on each dice, there are six dots.

Sequencing and conservation of numbers

Understanding sequences of numbers helps children recognize patterns and make sense of the world.

For example, a student fills out the missing numbers in the picture below.

1		3			6		8		10

Conservation of numbers means that a person is able to understand that the number of objects remains the same even when rearranged.

For example, the objects below all represent 4 objects regardless of how they are arranged.

Simple directions related to position and proximity

Students should be able relate positions using proximity. Below is an example.

Describe the position of the square in the picture below.

The square smaller and is above the triangle.

Represents numbers in multiple ways

Students in early childhood grades will represent numbers in different ways: shapes, tallies, objects, words, etc. See the example below.

Uses counting and cardinality principles

There are five long-established counting principles that children must know in order to be able to count well. These five counting principles are:

1. **Stable order** – Understanding the verbal sequence of counting; being able to say the number names in sequential order

2. **One-to-One correspondence** – Understanding that when saying the names of the numbers in sequence, each object receives one count and one only one count

3. **Cardinality** – Understanding that the last number spoken in a counting sequence names the quantity for that set

4. **Abstraction** – Understanding that no matter what the student is counting, how the student counts stays the same. For example, any set of objects can be counted as a set, regardless of whether they are the same color, shape, size, etc. This can also include non-physical things such as sounds, imaginary objects, etc.

5. **Order irrelevance** – Knowledge that the order that items are counted in is irrelevant—left-to-right, right-to-left, in a random fashion—as long as every object in the set is given one count and only one count.

(Gelman and Galistel, 1978)

Manipulatives (physical models)

Manipulatives are used to represent counting, patterns, operations, physical attributes of geometric figures, and formulas. It's not enough to know that snap cubes exist; you also need to be aware of how they are used. Below is a list of commonly used manipulatives.

1. **Attribute blocks** come in five different geometric shapes and different colors. Attribute blocks can be used for sorting, patterns, and teaching attributes of geometric figures.

2. **Base-10 blocks** are visual models in powers of 10 that represent ones, tens, hundreds, and thousands. These blocks can be used to teach place value, regrouping with addition or subtraction, fractions, decimals, percents, and area and volume.

3. **Bar diagrams** are used to represent parts and whole and are often used with finding a missing value in a number sentence (e.g.,).

4. **Counters** come in different shapes and colors (e.g., bears, bugs, chips) and are used for sorting and counting.

5. **Geoboards** are pegboard grids to which students stretch rubber bands to make geometric shapes. They are used to teach basic shapes, symmetry, congruency, perimeter, and area.

6. **Fraction strips** help to show the relationship between the numerator (top number of a fraction) and denominator (bottom number of a fraction) of a fraction and how parts relate to the whole.

7. **Snap cubes** are cubes that come in various colors that can be snapped together from any face. Snap cubes can be used to teach number sense, basic operations, counting, patterns, and place value.

8. **Tiles** are 1-inch squares that come in different colors. Some of the topics tiles can be used as a teaching aide include counting, estimating, place value, multiplication, fractions, and probability.

Manipulative Representations		
Attribute blocks	<ul><li>Sorting</li><li>Patterns</li><li>Attributes of figures</li></ul>	
Base-10 blocks	<ul><li>Place value</li><li>Whole number operations</li><li>Comparing numbers</li><li>Regrouping with addition and subtraction</li><li>Area and volume</li></ul>	
Bar diagram	<ul><li>Solve for an unknown value using one of the four operations</li><li>Solve word problems</li></ul>	Kelly added 5 more stamps to her collection. Now she has 24 stamps. How many did she have before? 18 | ? | 6 |
Counters	<ul><li>Sorting</li><li>Counting</li></ul>	
Geoboard	<ul><li>Perimeter</li><li>Area</li><li>Properties of basic shapes</li><li>Congruency and Similarity</li></ul>	

Manipulative Representations		
Fraction strips	• Perform operations with fractions • Represent fractional parts	<table><tr><td colspan="8" align="center">1</td></tr><tr><td colspan="4" align="center">$^1/_2$</td><td colspan="4" align="center">$^1/_2$</td></tr><tr><td colspan="2" align="center">$^1/_4$</td><td colspan="2" align="center">$^1/_4$</td><td colspan="2" align="center">$^1/_4$</td><td colspan="2" align="center">$^1/_4$</td></tr><tr><td>$^1/_8$</td><td>$^1/_8$</td><td>$^1/_8$</td><td>$^1/_8$</td><td>$^1/_8$</td><td>$^1/_8$</td><td>$^1/_8$</td><td>$^1/_8$</td></tr></table> $^1/_2 = {}^1/_4 + {}^1/_4 = {}^1/_8 + {}^1/_8 + {}^1/_8 + {}^1/_8$
Snap cubes	• Combine like terms • Represent ratios • Distributive property • Multiply polynomials • Factoring polynomials	
Tiles	• Perform operations with fractions • Represent fractional parts	

Quick Tip

Remember, in the early grades, students go from concrete thinking to abstract reasoning. They have to start by physically touching objects and understanding them in a concrete manner before they can understand them in an abstract manner.

This page intentionally left blank.

B – Numbers and Operations: Whole Numbers

1. Place-value system
2. Mental math strategies
3. Operations and properties involving whole numbers

1. Place-value system

Place value

The value of a certain digit is determined by the place it resides in a number. In our number system, each "place" has a value of ten times the place to its right or $\frac{1}{10}$ of the number to its left. The place value of each digit in a number is included in the word form of a number.

Take the number, 2,487,905.631, as an example.

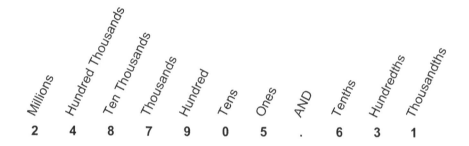

This number is read as two million, four hundred eighty-seven thousand, nine hundred five, and six hundred thirty-one thousandths.

Knowledge of place value helps students to compose and decompose larger numbers to better understand the size of the number.

It is important to know how to manipulate a number using the base 10 system. Moving the decimal point to the left (to create a smaller number), is the same as dividing by increments of 10 or multiplying by increments of $\frac{1}{10}$. Conversely, moving the decimal point to the right (to create a larger number) is the same as multiplying by increments of 10. Increments of 10 include 10, 100, 1000, 10,000…etc.

Knowledge of place value helps students to compose and decompose larger numbers to better understand the size of the number.

Example Question

Select all of the statements that are true about the number below.

340

    A. 3 is in the hundreds place.

    B. There are no 10s in this number.

    C. There is a zero in the one's place.

    D. 4 represents 40 in this number.

Correct answer: A, C, and D

The 3 is in the hundreds place, representing 300. There are 10s in this number, 4 of them to be exact. The one's place is occupied by a zero. 4 is in the 10's place which represents 40.

Expanded form

Another way to teach place value is by writing numbers in expanded form. A number written in **expanded form** is written so that the place value of each number is represented as part of a sum.

For example, the number **872** written in expanded form would be **800 + 70 + 2.**

An extension of expanded form is **expanded notation** where each digit is written as a product of its place value. The number 872 written in expanded notation would be $(8 \times 100) + (7 \times 10) + (2 \times 1)$..

Example Question

Write the number 453 in expanded form.

    A. 4 + 5 + 3

    B. 40 + 50 + 3

    C. 400 + 50 + 3

    D. 453 + 0

Correct Answer: C

The 4 is in the hundred's, the 5 is in the ten's place, and 3 is in the one's place, making the expanded form: 400 + 50 + 3.

Estimation

Estimation is a strategy used to find a quick answer that is close to the actual answer and to check the reasonableness of a solution. Finding a rough calculation or approximation using different estimation strategies are helpful in different situations. The following table lists three ways to estimate a solution.

Strategy	Example
Compatible numbers	Estimating by rounding pairs of numbers to numbers that are easy to add, subtract, multiply, or divide. Example: becomes so the estimated value is
Clustering	Estimating sums or products when all the numbers are close to a single value. Example: becomes so the estimated value is .
Front-end estimation	Estimating by rounding to the greatest place value or the number in front. Example: would become , so the estimated value is

Quick Tip

Test questions may use terms that are part of a basic operation problem. Know what each of these terms mean. Vocabulary terms used most often include:

- **Addend** – a number added to another. For example, in the problem 4 + 2 = 6, the numbers 4 and 2 are addends.

- **Sum** – the total number after 2 or more numbers are added together. For example, in the problem 4 + 2 = 6, the number 6 is the sum.

- **Difference** – the change in a number after subtraction. For example, in the problem 6 – 4 = 2, the difference is 2.

- **Product** – the result of multiplying numbers. For example, in the problem 4 × 2 = 8, the product is 8.

- **Quotient** – the result of dividing one number by another. For example, in the problem 8 ÷ 2 = 4, the quotient is 4.

2. Mental math strategies

Inventive strategies are methods in which students invent ways to solve complex problems. They involve using reason and understanding to get to the end result. Here are some examples of inventive strategies students use:

- **Partitioning.** Taking large numbers and splitting them into small, manageable units.

- **Compensation.** Borrowing pieces of one number to compensate for another to make it easier to solve.

Standard algorithm is a specific method of computation that is conventionally taught for solving particular mathematical problem using standard notation in:

Partitioning	Compensation
467 – 122 =	46 + 38 =
400 – 100 = 300	Take **4** from **38** and give it to **46**.
60 – 20 = 40	
7 – 2 = 5	50 + 34 =
345	**84**

- Exchanging

- Regrouping

- Long division

- Long multiplication

- Average

- Area

- Volume

3. Operations and properties involving whole numbers

When learning to add and subtract in kindergarten through second grade, students learn to approach a problem from different points of view. Various points of view help the student to better understand operations and number facts and is also preparing them for solving for an unknown value in later grades.

Add to

A number is given, and more is being added to the number to find a **sum**.

Result Unknown	Change Unknown	Start Unknown
Jon had two books. Kevin gave him 4 more books. How many books does Jon have now? $$2 + 4 = ?$$	Manda has three pencils. She found some more pencils in her room. Now she has seven pencils. How many pencils did she find in her room? $$3 + ? = 7$$	There are some birds resting on a fountain wall. Two more birds just joined them. Now there are five birds. How many birds were there on the wall to start? $$? + 2 = 5$$

Take from

A number is given, and some is being taken from this number to find a **difference**.

Result Unknown	Change Unknown	Start Unknown
Tory had five pieces of candy. She gave away 2 pieces. How many pieces does she have now? $$5 - 2 = ?$$	Six baseballs were on the ground. Evan picked some of them up to throw to a friend. There were three balls still on the ground. How many baseballs did Evan take? $$6 - ? = 3$$	There were some cookies on a plate. Scotty ate four of the cookies. Then there was one cookie on the plate. How many cookies were on the plate before Scott ate some? $$? - 4 = 1$$

Put together and take apart

This is often referred to as part-part-whole. Part of the number is given, then another part is given to make a total amount.

Total Unknown	Addend Unknown	Both Addends Unknown
There were four cups on the table. Jamie put one more cup on the table. How many cups are on the table? $$4 + 1 = ?$$	Darrell has seven pairs of socks. Three pair are blue, and the rest are white. How many pairs of socks are white? $$3 + ? = 7$$ $$7 - 3 = ?$$	Brock has four tickets to place into two buckets, bucket A and bucket B. How many tickets can he put in A, and how many can he put in B? $$? + ? = 4$$ $1 + 3$ and $3 + 1$ are different when listing all the possibilities.

Compare addition and subtraction

Two values are given for a total, with the size of one being compared to the size of the other.

Difference Unknown	Bigger Unknown	Smaller Unknown
How many more?	**"More" Version**	**"More" Version**
There are five butterflies on a purple flowering bush. There are three butterflies on a yellow flowering bush. How many more butterflies are on the purple flowering bush? $3 + ? = 5$	Tory has four more tickets than Paula. Paula has 3 tickets. How many tickets does Tory have? $3 + 4 = ?$	Joseph has two more dollars than Stephen. Joseph has five dollars. How many dollars does Stephen have? $5 - 2 = ?$
How many fewer?	**"Fewer" Version**	**"Fewer" Version**
Kevon has three oranges. Natasha has six oranges. How many fewer oranges does Kevon have than Natasha? $6 - 3 = ?$	Elvin has one fewer notebook than Josiah. Elvin has four notebooks. How many notebooks does Josiah have? $? - 1 = 4$	Petra has three fewer fish than Deana. Deana has eight fish. How many fish does Petra have? $? + 3 = 8$

Equal groups

Beginning in third grade, students work with multiplication and division as an extension of addition and subtraction. The tables that follow outline how students learn multiplication and division. Be familiar with the terms in the chart and the type and composition of problems that each scenario represents.

Unknown Product	Group Size Unknown	Number of Groups Unknown
Multiplication	**How many in each group?** **Division**	**How many groups?** **Division**
There are 3 bags with 6 plums in each bag. How many plums are there in all? $3 \times 6 = ?$	If 18 plums are shared equally into 3 bags, then how many plums will be in each bag? $3 \times ? = 18$ and $18 \div 3 = ?$	If 18 plums are to be packed 6 to a bag, then how many bags are needed? $? \times 6 = 18$ and $18 \div 6 = ?$
Measurement Example	Measurement Example	Measurement Example
You need 4 lengths of string, each 5 inches long. How much string will you need altogether? $4 \times 5 = ?$	You have 12 inches of string, which you will cut into 6 equal pieces. How long will each piece of string be? $6 \times ? = 12$ and $12 \div 6 = ?$	You have 14 inches of string, which you will cut into pieces that are 7 inches long. How many pieces of string will you have? $? \times 7 = 14$ and $14 \div 7 = ?$

Arrays and area

Unknown Product	Group Size Unknown	Number of Groups Unknown
Array Example	Array Example	Array Example
There are 3 rows of apples with 6 apples in each row. How many apples are there? $$3 \times 6 = ?$$	If 18 apples are arranged into 3 equal rows, how many apples will be in each row? $$3 \times ? = 18 \text{ and } 18 \div 3 = ?$$	If 18 apples are arranged into equal rows of 6 apples, how many rows will there be? $$? \times 6 = 18 \text{ and } 18 \div 6 = ?$$
Area Example	Area Example	Area Example
What is the area of a 4 cm by 5 cm rectangle? $$4 \times 5 = ?$$	A rectangle has area 12 square centimeters. If one side is 6 cm long, how long is a side next to it? $$6 \times ? = 12 \text{ and } 12 \div 6 = ?$$	A rectangle has area 14 square centimeters. If one side is 7 cm long, how long is a side next to it? $$? \times 7 = 14 \text{ and } 14 \div 7 = ?$$

II. MATHEMATICS

C – Numbers and Operations: Fractions

1. Multiple representations and meanings of fractions

2. Working with rational fractions

1. Multiple representations and meanings of fractions

Proportional relationships

A **ratio** is a comparison of two numbers using a fraction, a colon, or the word "to". **Rates** are ratios with different units, while ratios have the same units. Rates are often expressed as unit rates and are read using the word "per" instead of "to." It is common to reference a unit rate in everyday language.

Rates and Ratios	
Verbal statement	Four dogs for every three cats
Manipulatives/picture	
Fraction	$\dfrac{4 \text{ dogs}}{3 \text{ cats}}$
Colon	4 dogs: 3 cats OR 4:3

A **unit rate** is a rate with a denominator of 1. Examples of unit rates include 60 miles per hour $\left(\dfrac{60 \text{ miles}}{1 \text{ hour}}\right)$, \$3 per box $\left(\dfrac{\$3}{1 \text{ box}}\right)$, or 22 students per teacher $\left(\dfrac{22 \text{ students}}{1 \text{ teacher}}\right)$. Any rate can be converted to a unit rate by dividing the numerator of the fraction by the denominator.

When two ratios are equivalent, they can be set equal to one another to form a **proportion**.

2. Working with rational fractions

Students learn unit fractions using fractional pieces of circles or bars and also by breaking up a number line into fractional pieces. From the number line, students learn the placement of fractions and their size relative to one another and to 0 and 1. The table that follows gives examples of some, not all, unit fractions.

Unit Fraction	Manipulative Representation	Number Line Representation
$\frac{1}{2}$	or	The fraction $\frac{1}{2}$ is the same distance from both 0 and 1.
$\frac{1}{4}$	or	The fraction $\frac{1}{4}$ is closer to 0 than 1, and $\frac{1}{4}$ is less than $\frac{1}{2}$
$\frac{1}{5}$	or	The fraction $\frac{2}{5}$ is closer to 0 than 1, and $\frac{3}{5}$ is greater than $\frac{1}{2}$

Working with unit fractions leads to decomposing fractions and writing an equation to represent the decomposition. To **decompose** a fraction means to break it into parts.

Example question

Which of the following is a decomposition of $\frac{3}{4}$?

A. $\frac{1}{4} + \frac{1}{4} + \frac{1}{4} = \frac{3}{4}$

B. $\frac{3}{4} = 0.75 = 75\%$

C. $\frac{1}{4} + \frac{3}{4} = \frac{4}{4} = 1$

D. $\frac{1}{2} < \frac{3}{4}$

Correct answer: A

Decomposing a fraction means to break a fraction up into the sum of smaller parts with the same denominator. Options B, C, and D do not break the fraction into smaller parts.

Number representation

The same number can be written several ways. Be prepared to know how to write a number in different forms or recognize equivalent forms of the same number. Also, be prepared to compare numbers written in different forms.

Fractions, decimals, and percents are all interchangeable and are acceptable in any of the three forms. Each of these is a number out of 100, so base-10 blocks create an effective visual when first learning percents and decimals.

Form	Example
Base-10 blocks	When interchanging fractions, decimals, and percents, we think of this out of 100. To represent this pictorially, we can use a base-10 block with 100 squares. The image to the right has 30 squares shaded or 30 out of 100, which is $\frac{30}{100}$
Fraction	The fraction $\frac{30}{100}$ may also be written as $\frac{3}{10}$.
Decimal	To convert a fraction to a decimal, always divide the numerator (top number) by the denominator (bottom number); numerator ÷ denominator. $30 \div 100 = 0.30$ or 0.3
Percent	To convert a decimal to a percent, move the decimal point 2 place values to the right. This works because a fraction and its decimal are out of 1, and a percent is out of 100. Moving the decimal point two places to the right is the same as multiplying by 100. **Example:** To convert 0.30 to a percent, move the decimal 2 places to the right: $0.30 = 30\%$ This is the same as $0.30 \times 100 = 30$. Moving the decimal is the shortcut; make sure you always know the math behind the shortcuts.

Application problems for fraction, decimal, and percent conversions often include having to find the percent of a number. To find **the percent of a number**, change the percent to a decimal and multiply the decimal by the number. For example, of is .

Example question

Choose a number from the list that is greater than 70% but less than 80%. Write your answer in the box.

A. 0.85

B. $\frac{65}{100}$

C. 1

D. 0.75

Correct response: D

To solve, rewrite each of the numbers as a decimal so that they are easy to compare.

$70\% = 0.7$

$80\% = 0.8$

The correct choice should be between 0.7 and 0.8.

0.85 is greater than 0.8 so answer choice A can be eliminated.

$\frac{65}{100} = 0.65$ is less than 0.7 so answer choice B can be eliminated.

1 is greater than 0.8 so answer choice C can be eliminated.

0.75 is between 0.7 and 0.8 so answer choice D is the correct answer.

Example question

Which of the following expressions is equivalent to 0.75. Select all that apply.

   A. $\dfrac{75}{100}$

   B. $\dfrac{3}{5}$

   C. 75%

   D. $5^2 + 50$

   E. 0.750

   F. $1 - \dfrac{1}{4}$

Correct response: A, C, E, F

To solve, rewrite each of the numbers as a decimal so that they are easy to compare.

$\dfrac{75}{100} = 0.75$

$\dfrac{3}{5} = 0.6$

$75\% = 0.75$

$5^2 + 50 = 25 + 50 = 75$

$0.750 = 0.75$

$1 - \dfrac{1}{4} = \dfrac{3}{4} = 0.75$

D – Algebraic Thinking

1. Working with patterns
2. Properties of operations

1. Working with patterns

When teaching addition, teachers can use a variety hands-on tools. When teaching basic addition and addition with regrouping, snap cubes or similar manipulatives are effective visual models to show groups of ten, how to regroup, and why we "carry" when a sum is greater than 9. As students become more proficient with addition, number lines provide a more numeric visual of addition and subtraction and will be used again when students work with integer operations.

Before students memorize multiplication facts, understanding that multiplication is repeated addition by modeling with groups and arrays helps to build a strong foundation. An **array** is an organized arrangement of the same number of objects in rows. The first number in a multiplication problem defines the number of rows, and the second number defines how many objects are in the row. For the multiplication problem , the array would contain 3 rows of 5 objects.

You may have to identify appropriate manipulatives for an operation or may be asked to identify the problem the manipulative is modeling. You may also be asked to identify an array that appropriately represents multiplication.

Example: Model the problem below using both a manipulative and a number line.

Dory has 5 books. Kelvin gives her 4 more books. How many books does Dory have now?

Solution: This problem is an add-to problem where the total is unknown. Using snap cubes, we can start with 5 and then add 4 more to the 5 to find the total. Students conclude that there are 9 total cubes.

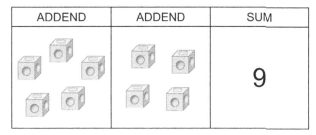

Using a number line, start with the first addend, 5, then move 4 spaces right to find the total number of books.

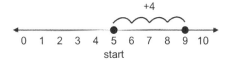

Example: Use groups and arrays to model the problem below.

Tina ordered 4 boxes of tennis balls. Each box contains 3 tennis balls. How many tennis balls did Tina order?

Solution: To use groups, show 3 tennis balls in each of the 4 boxes. Students should see that repeated addition is the same as multiplication and 4 groups of 3 is 12.

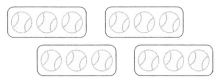

An array puts groups into organized lines, preparing students for additional math topics, such as area. The process and result are the same as with the groups. There are 4 rows of 3 tennis balls each, which is 12 tennis balls.

There may be problems that require you to find the percent of a number. The percent should be a value that is easy to calculate because you will not have a calculator. When having to compute the percent of a number mentally or by hand, it is helpful to find 10% of the number and use this value to calculate 15% or 20%.

For example, if you have to find 20% of a $42 item, first find 10% by moving the decimal point one place to the left. 10% of $42 is $4.20. Because 20% is the same as having 10% twice, double the value you got for 10%. $4.20 doubled is $8.40.

If you have to find 15% of $42, start with 10%, or $4.20. Because 15% is 10% plus another 5%, or half of 10%, take half of $4.20 for the remaining 5%. This is $2.10. Thus 15% is $4.20 plus $2.10 or $6.30.

Area model

Area models, linear models, and set models are different ways to physically represent fraction problems.

In an area model, fractions are represented as part of a region. Think of a 10 by 10 grid with some of the squares shaded. The shaded squares represent a fractional part of the whole.

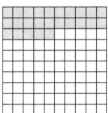

Linear model

In a linear model, the lengths of objects are compared to one another.

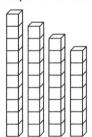

For example, think about 4 red snap cubes snapped together in a row and three green snap cubes snapped together to form another row. The green cubes are $\frac{3}{4}$ the length of the red cubes.

Set model

In a set model, a number of individual objects make up one whole.

For example, 8 two color counters could make up 1 set of counters; then 4 counters would represent $\frac{4}{8}$ or $\frac{1}{2}$ of the set.

2. Properties of operations

Know the properties of operations for the exam, including how and when they are used. As students become more proficient with addition and multiplication, these properties allow them to fluently change and simplify problems.

Property of Operations	Rule	Description
Commutative Property of Addition	$a + b = b + a$	Changing the order of two numbers being added does not change the sum.
Commutative Property of Multiplication	$a \cdot b = b \cdot a$	Changing the order of two numbers being multiplied does not change the product.
Associative Property of Addition	$(a + b) + c = a + (b + c)$	Changing the grouping of the addends does not change the sum.
Associative Property of Multiplication	$a \cdot (b \cdot c) = (a \cdot b) \cdot c$	Changing the grouping of the factors does not change the product.
Additive Identity Property of 0	$a + 0 = 0 + a = a$	Adding 0 to a number does not change the value of that number.
Multiplicative Identity Property of 1	$a \cdot 1 = 1 \cdot a = a$	Multiplying a number by 1 does not change the value of that number.
Inverse Property of Addition	For every a, there exists a number $-a$ such that $a + (-a) = (-a) + a = 0$	Adding a number and its opposite results in a sum equal to 0.
Inverse Property of Multiplication	For every a, there exists a number $\frac{1}{a}$ such that $a \cdot \frac{1}{a} = \frac{1}{a} \cdot a = \frac{a}{a} = 1$	Multiplying a number and its multiplicative inverse results in a product equal to 1.

Property of Operations	Rule	Description
Distributive Property of Multiplication over Addition	$a \cdot (b + c) = a \cdot b + a \cdot c$	Multiplying a sum is the same as multiplying each addend by that number, then adding their products.
Distributive Property of Multiplication over Subtraction	$a \cdot (b - c) = a \cdot b - a \cdot c$	Multiplying a difference is the same as multiplying the minuend and subtrahend by that number, then subtracting their products.
Transitivity Property	$x = y$ and $y = z$, then $x = z$	For all real numbers x, y, and z, if $x = y$ and $y = z$, then $x = z$. If $x = y$, then x may be replaced by y in any equation or expression.

The acronym, PEMDAS, or the mnemonic *Please Excuse My Dear Aunt Sally*, is often used to remember the order of operations.

Please, or parentheses, includes all grouping symbols, which may include brackets [ ], braces { }, and absolute value bars | |. If there is math that can be computed inside grouping symbols, do that FIRST, then the grouping symbols may be removed.

Excuse, or exponents, means anything raised to a power should be simplified after there are no more parentheses.

My **D**ear, or multiplication or division, are essentially the same "type" of operation and are therefore done in order from left to right, just as you would read a book. All multiplication and division should be completed BEFORE any addition or subtraction that is not inside parentheses.

Aunt **S**ally, or addition and subtraction, are also essentially the same "type" of operation and are also done in order from left to right. These operations should always come last, unless they were inside parentheses.

P	**Parentheses**
E	**Exponents**
M D	**Multiplication & Division**
A S	**Addition & Subtraction**

Example question

Simplify the expression.

$(16 - 4) \div (5 - 2)$

   A. 1

   B. 2

   C. 4

   D. 8

Correct answer: C

$(\underline{16 - 4}) \div (\underline{5 - 2})$

$= 12 \div 3$

$= 4$

E – Geometry, Measurement, and Data

1. Shape attributes
2. Measurement and estimation using standard and nonstandard units of measure
3. Representing and interpreting data

1. Shape attributes

Figure Name	Image	Attributes
Rectangle		• All angles equal 90° • Opposite sides have the same length • A special type of parallelogram • Opposite sides are parallel
Square		• All angles equal 90° • All sides have the same length • A special type of parallelogram • A special type of rectangle • Opposite sides are parallel
Circle		• Diameter goes through the center of the circle to the edge of the circle • Radius starts at the center of the circle and ends on the edge of the circle • The radius is half the length of the diameter.
Cube		• All sides of a cube are squares • All sides have the same length • All angles equal 90°

Figure	Name	Number of Sides
	Triangle	3
	Rectangle	4
	Square	4

Figure	Name	Number of Sides
	Pentagon	5
	Hexagon	6
	Heptagon	7
	Octagon	8

The table that follows lists the name of prisms and pyramids and gives an example of a possible net. Sometimes the figure is turned on its side, and the bases are located on the sides of the figure (see the rectangular prism and triangular figures in the table).

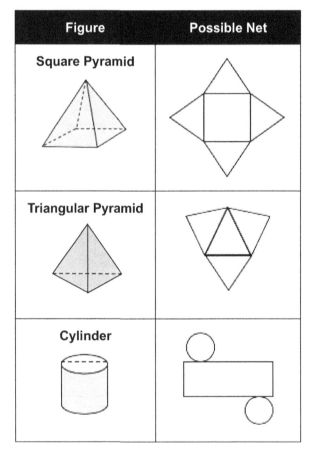

Figure	Possible Net
Rectangular Prism	
Cube	
Triangular Prism	

Figure	Possible Net
Square Pyramid	
Triangular Pyramid	
Cylinder	

2. Measurement and estimation using standard and nonstandard units of measure

The measurement portion of the test includes conversions within the U.S. customary system, conversions within the metric system, and an understanding of the relative size of basic measurements. You may be asked what measurement would be used to measure the weight, length, or capacity of an object, so you should have an understanding of the relative size of each unit. The examples in the table should help you understand the size of the units.

<table>
<tr><th colspan="2">U.S. Customary System</th></tr>
<tr><th>Units</th><th>Realistic Use</th></tr>
<tr><td>Inches</td><td>Length of a pencil
Length of a person's hand</td></tr>
<tr><td>Feet</td><td>Height of a door
Length of a car</td></tr>
<tr><td>Yards</td><td>Length of a football field
A yard is about 1 meter</td></tr>
<tr><td>Miles</td><td>Length of a river
Distance between cities</td></tr>
<tr><td>Pint</td><td>Beer glass
Small tub of ice cream</td></tr>
<tr><td>Quart</td><td>Bottle of motor oil
A quart is about 1 liter</td></tr>
<tr><td>Gallons</td><td>Large milk jug
Gasoline</td></tr>
<tr><td>Ounces (weight)</td><td>Weight of a block of cheese
Weight of a paperback book</td></tr>
<tr><td>Pounds</td><td>Weight of a person
Weight of a packed suitcase</td></tr>
<tr><td>Tons</td><td>Weight of a car
Weight of a plane</td></tr>
</table>

<table>
<tr><th colspan="2">Metric System</th></tr>
<tr><th>Units</th><th>Realistic Use</th></tr>
<tr><td>Meter</td><td>Length around a track
Length of a large swimming pool</td></tr>
<tr><td>Liter</td><td>Large bottle of soda
Bottle of shampoo</td></tr>
<tr><td>Gram</td><td>Weight of a paperclip</td></tr>
<tr><td>Centimeter</td><td>Height of a person
Length of a textbook</td></tr>
<tr><td>Kilometer</td><td>Driving distances</td></tr>
<tr><td>Milliliter</td><td>Liquid medications</td></tr>
<tr><td>Kilogram</td><td>Weight of a person
Weight of a box of paper</td></tr>
</table>

The measurement portion of the test includes conversions within the U.S. customary system, conversions within the metric system, and an understanding of the relative size of basic measurements.

Metric conversions

The metric system is based on units of 10. When converting within the metric system, you are only responsible for the basic units: kilo-, centi-, and milli-. The other units that are grayed out are to show the conversions by units of 10.

Metric Conversions						
Prefixes						
Kilo-	Hecto-	Deca-	**Basic Unit**	Deci-	**Centi-**	**Milli-**
Abbreviations						
km	hm	dkm	**meter (m)**	dm	**cm**	**mm**
kL	hL	dkL	**liter (L)**	dL	**cL**	**mL**
kg	hg	dkg	**gram (g)**	dg	**cg**	**mg**
0.001	0.01	0.1	**1**	10	**100**	**1,000**

There are two different ways to approach metric conversions: moving the decimal and using a proportion.

Convert by moving the decimal point.

If the conversion is from a **smaller unit to a larger unit**, move the decimal point **LEFT** the number of spaces between the two units.

If the conversion if from a **larger unit to a smaller unit**, move the decimal point **RIGHT** the number of spaces between the two units.

This method requires memorizing the abbreviations in order.

Example question

Complete the following.

4.5 L = _____ kL

    A. 0.0045 kL

    B. 45000 kL

    C. 450 kL

    D. 0.045 kL

Correct response: A

The conversion is going from a smaller unit to a larger unit. Therefore, the decimal point moves to the left. Liters is 3 units away from kiloliters, so the decimal point moves three places to the left.

kiloliter   hectoliter   decaliter   liter

You can also solve this by setting up a proportion.

Example question

Complete the following. 4 km = _____ mm

    A. 400 mm

    B. 0.4000 mm

    C. 4,000,000 mm

    D. 0.0004 mm

Correct answer: C

The conversion is going from a larger unit to a smaller unit. Therefore, the decimal point moves to the right. Kilometers and millimeters are six units apart, so the decimal point moves six places to the right.

4 km = 4,000,000 mm

Convert using a proportion.

To use a proportion, create a ratio from the problem, and set up an equivalent ratio using the numbers in the table.

This method requires memorizing the abbreviations in order and knowing how to add in the numerical values.

Example question

Complete the following. 4L = _____ mL

    A. 40 mL

    B. 4000 mL

    C. 4,000,000 mL

    D. 0.0004 mL

Correct answer: B

The ratio created from the problem is $\dfrac{4L}{x \text{ mL}}$, and the ratio created from the table would be $\dfrac{1L}{1000 \text{ mL}}$.

Choose the units from the problem to determine the units for the second ratio. The proportion would be:

$$\frac{4L}{x \text{ mL}} = \frac{1L}{1000 \text{ mL}}$$

Cross-multiply and solve.

$4000 = 1x$

Standard conversions

Standard conversions require quite a bit of straight memorization, which is not the purpose of the exam. It is not likely (of course anything is possible) that a question asks for conversions across multiple units, such as cups to gallons.

Standard US Conversions	
1 foot = 12 inches	1 cup = 8 fluid ounces
1 yard = 3 feet = 36 inches	1 pint = 2 cups
1 mile = 5,280 feet = 1760 yards	1 quart = 2 pints
1 hour = 60 minutes	1 gallon = 4 quarts
1 minute = 60 seconds	1 pound = 16 ounces
	1 ton = 2,000 pounds

Standard conversions are often embedded in questions that contain measurements in two units but require only one unit to solve. For example, finding the area of a square that measures 8 inches by 2 feet.

3. Representing and interpreting data

Starting at a young age, students are expected to collect, organize, and represent data. Students do this by understanding pictographs, bar graphs, and circle or pie charts.

Pictograph

A pictograph is a graph that uses pictures to represent numerical data. The visual representation of data on a pictograph allows for quick identification of the mode and distribution of the data set. A key is important for a pictograph so that the reader of the graph knows what each picture represents.

Example question

Based on the data provided, how many more people bought a tree on Friday than on Tuesday?

🌲 = 10 trees

🌲 = 5 trees

Answer:

Friday's trees = 75

Tuesday's trees = 30

75 − 30 = 45

45 more people bought trees on Friday than Tuesday.

Day	Number of Trees Sold
Monday	🌲 🌲 🌲 🌲
Tuesday	🌲 🌲 🌲
Wednesday	🌲 🌲 🌲 🌲 🌲
Thursday	🌲 🌲 🌲 🌲
Friday	🌲 🌲 🌲 🌲 🌲 🌲 🌲
Saturday	🌲 🌲 🌲 🌲 🌲 🌲 🌲 🌲 🌲

Bar graph

A bar graph is typically used to track and compare change over time. The bars in a bar graph can be close together but should not touch. Examples of when a bar graph might be used to display data include:

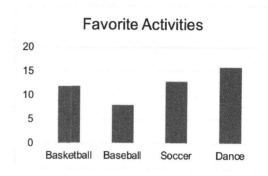

- Total electric bill for each high school in the county during the month of June

- Number of students enrolled in 7th grade advanced math over the last six years

- Students' favorite sports activities during the school year

A bar graph may be used to compare the same data for more than one set of data on the same display.

Circle graph

A circle graph, sometimes called a pie chart, is a visual representation that best shows proportional relationships. The data is presented in percentages and compares parts to a whole. What percent of a budget is used to pay various bills is an example of proportional data that could be displayed in a circle graph.

Data	Graph
A recent survey asked 500 high school students about the number of televisions in their house. The percent of students answering 1, 2, 3, or 4 or more are in the table below. <table><tr><td>**Number of TVs**</td><td>**Percent**</td></tr><tr><td>1</td><td>10</td></tr><tr><td>2</td><td>15</td></tr><tr><td>3</td><td>20</td></tr><tr><td>4 or more</td><td>55</td></tr></table> Once data is collected, find the percent of the total for each category. Use this percent to find the number of degrees out of the 360 degrees in a circle that each part of the survey represents (the size of each piece of the pie).	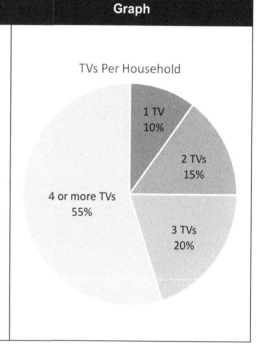

Venn diagram

Data in a Venn diagram is categorical data, meaning that the data falls into specific categories. Venn diagrams are used to show relationships among sets using overlapping circles to depict relationships. Any relationships that overlap are counted in the region where the circles of the diagram also overlap (Overlapping data is when data falls in more than one category). Venn diagrams are useful for depicting the likelihood of an event occurring and for making comparisons.

Data in Venn diagrams is often referred to using the terms union and intersection.

Union, represented by the symbol , is all the data in two or more sets put together.

Intersection, represented by the symbol , is only where two or more data sets overlap.

Data	Graph
Math only certification: 42 Science only certification: 28 Math and science certification: 8 To graph, create a circle for each category. Data that does not overlap stays outside the overlap. Data that includes both categories should be in the overlap section.	

Mathematics Practice Questions

1. A teacher is using dice to help students recognize numbers. She rolls one di, and the students immediately say, "Three!" What skill are the students and teacher working on?

   A. Transitivity

   B. Patterns

   C. Subitizing

   D. Decomposition

2. Which of the following would be most appropriate for helping students to recognize patterns?

   A.

   C.

   B.

   D.

3. A teacher is helping students work towards the objective of classifying and categorizing geometric shapes. Which prerequisite skill must students master before they can meet this new objective?

   A. Defining area

   B. Drawing shapes

   C. Recognizing shape attributes

   D. Identifying patterns

4. A teacher is working with students on units of measurement. What would be the most effective activity to meet the objective below?

   Students will use nonstandard units of measure to calculate length.

   A. Have students measure their desks using paperclips.

   B. Have students form a line from tallest student to shortest student.

   C. Have students use a tape measure to measure the length and width of the room.

   D. Have students work in cooperative groups to read about standard units of measure.

5. A teacher has students pick their favorite animal out of a group of 4 animals: dog, dolphin, frog elephant. Then students create the chart below based on everyone's preference. What skill does this activity reinforce?

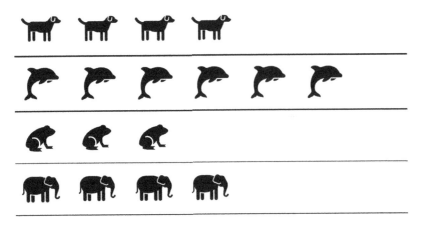

A. Pattern recognition

B. Decomposition of numbers

C. Data organization

D. Probability

6. The manipulative below would be most effective in reinforcing what skill in students?

A. Fractions

B. Order

C. Patterns

D. Base ten

7. A teacher is using the following word problem with students. Which skill does this word problem reinforce?

Jan has 7 pieces of gum in her backpack. Sidney has 4 pieces in his backpack. How many more pieces of gum does Jan have than Sidney has.

A. Addition

B. Subtraction

C. Multiplication

D. Division

8. A teacher is using the number below and asks, "What is the value of the underline number?"

345

What skill is the teacher working on?

A. Multidigit numbers

B. Estimation

C. Subitizing

D. Place value

9. A teacher has students use the diagram below to represent 25%. In this lesson, what skill is the teacher focusing on?

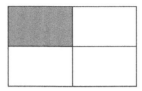

A. Understanding fractions represent division problems

B. Understanding whole numbers can be decomposed to parts of numbers

C. Understanding equivalent fractions equal the same amount

D. Understanding fractions can be represented in a variety of ways

10. A teacher is showing students how to represent data in a variety of ways. She wants them to pick the most appropriate graph or chart to present a data set. Which of the following would be most appropriate for representing the percent of students who like various favors of ice cream—25% strawberry, 25% vanilla, and 50% chocolate?

A. Line graph

B. Bar graph

C. Pictograph

D. Circle graph

Number	Answer	Explanation
1.	C	Subitizing comes from the Latin word meaning suddenly. The term *subitize* refers to students' ability to immediately identify the number without counting.
2.	B	Answer B is the only choice out of the 4 options that shows a pattern.
3.	C	Before students can classify and categorize shapes, they must have the prerequisite skill of identifying and recognizing shape attributes.
4.	A	Using nonstandard units of measure means using something other than a ruler or tape measure to measure objects. Students measuring desks with paperclips or pencils is a common early childhood practice of using nonstandard units of measure.
5.	C	In this case, students are organizing data. They are putting all the different animals in order and organizing it in a way that they can see how many students like which animal. Organizing data is an essential early skill in math.
6.	A	This is a fraction strip representing .
7.	B	The phrase *how many more* in the question stem indicates subtraction. You must subtract Sidney's pieces from Jan's pieces, and you get a difference of 3 pieces.
8.	D	Place value is determining the number value of an underlined part of a multidigit number. In this case, the place value is 40 because the 4 is in the 10s place.
9.	D	In this case 25% and of the squares represent the same fraction in different ways.
10.	D	Pie charts or circle graphs are most effective in displaying percentages. The entire pie or circle represents 100%. Then each slice represents the pieces or percentages. This pie chart or circle graph would look like this:

III. Social Studies

This page intentionally left blank.

A – Identity, Social, and Emotional Development

1. Individual development, and relationships to others

1. Individual development, and relationships to others

Domains of Human Development

While all human development theorists built off of the work of their predecessors, emphasis is put on how they expand our understanding of social, physical, moral, and cognitive development. Cognitive, physical, social, and moral domains are described in stages of individual progress. Each stage has a range of typical variances because not all children progress at the same pace. In addition, it is possible for children to demonstrate characteristics across more than one stage of development at the same time. An atypical variance is when a child is far out of the expected age range – either above or below peers. It is important to document these atypical variances because they may be a sign a larger problem that will only be identified when a pattern of differences is observed.

Cognitive Development

Cognitive development involves thinking, reasoning, problem-solving, understanding. Jean Piaget is widely known for his stages of cognitive development. This is a framework for how students develop intellectually through various stages. Piaget asserted that cognitive development was a reorganization of mental processes resulting from biological maturation and environmental experience (1972).

Piaget's 4 Stages of Cognitive Development		
Sensorimotor	0–2 years	Children at this stage figure out the world through sensory and motor experiences. Object permanence and separation anxiety are hallmarks of this stage.
Pre-operational	2–6 years	Children at this stage identify and use symbols for objects but do not have the ability to apply logical reasoning. They know how to play pretend and are egocentric.
Concrete operational	7–12 years	Logical reasoning about concrete objects kicks in during this stage. Conservation, reversibility, serial ordering, and understanding cause and effect relationships are hallmarks of this stage, but thinking is still limited to the concrete.
Formal operational	12 years–adult	Abstract thinking such as logic, deductive reasoning, comparison, and classification are demonstrated by the individual in this stage.

Social Development

Social development involves interpersonal skills, initiating play, interactions with peers. Theorists like Vygotsky, Bandura, and Erikson are credited with theories in early childhood social development.

Lev Vygotsky stressed the fundamental role of social interaction in the development of cognition. He believed strongly that community plays a central role in the process of making meaning. Vygotsky is most widely known for the Zone of Proximal Development (ZPD), which he asserted is the distance between the actual developmental level as determined by independent problem solving and the level of potential development as determined through problem-solving under adult guidance, or in collaboration with more capable peers (Vygotsky, 1978). Helping someone move through the Zone of Proximal Development depends on 1) presences of a more knowledgeable person, 2) social interactions, and 3) scaffolding or supportive activities developed by the educator.

Albert Bandura is best known for his social learning theory on modeled behaviors or observational learning. He stressed that students learn from what they observe and that teachers can be proactive about how they demonstrate and promote behaviors. He asserted that students are more likely to emulate a behavior if they value the outcome and admire the modeler. His theory builds on the central elements of Vygotsky's learning theirs which also emphasize social learning. Bandura's social learning theory has four stages: attention (observation of modeled behaviors), retention (memory), motor reproduction (practice and replication of behaviors), and motivation (self-efficacy and personal motivation to use new behaviors). (Bandura, 1972)

Erik Erikson argues that development is determined by how a person is treated and the environment they inhabit. After that, he argues that a person's development is mostly impacted by a person's choices or how they react to external factors. In all stages, the context, which can be controlled, impacts growth and development.

Erikson in the early childhood classroom:

- Provide opportunities for students to participate more regularly in creating, building, modeling, and learning

- Encourage students to develop a sense of pride for their accomplishments and capability

- Give students responsibilities to develop ownership and independence

Lawrence Kohlberg built on Piaget's research to explore the development of morality and came up with 3 levels of morality with two stages at each level. He argued that everyone works through the stages sequentially but at varying rates, and not everyone reaches the highest stages. Understanding these stages of moral development is helpful when answering questions about norms and social behavior on the exam.

	Stages / Orientations	Explanation / Example
Level 1: Preconventional Morality Behaviors are based on perceived individual consequences. **ages 5-10+**	**Stage 1: Punishment and Obedience Orientation** A child's incentive to obey is to not be punished.	Did my mom say this is ok? What will happen if I take this cookie?
	Stage 2: Instrumental Purpose Orientation behavior based on receiving rewards or satisfying personal needs	Is this self-serving? Can I do this without an adult knowing?
Level 2 Conventional Morality Behaviors determined by the rules of adults, peers, and government **ages 10-15+**	**Stage 3 Good Boy/Nice Girl Orientation** behavior based on social approval	Am I following the school rules? Will my peers and teachers be happy with my actions?
	Stage 4: Law and Order Orientation behavior based on laws and social rules.	Individual begins to look beyond their own ties to the abstract, "greater good." They are more aware of laws, and social norms of society.

	Stages / Orientations	Explanation / Example
Level 3 Postconventional or Principled Morality Behaviors based on abstract principles and values. **Age 15+**	**Stage 5: Social Contract Orientation** When the individual feels they're in a conflict between personal rights and the law, exceptions are made.	Laws are not always clear-cut. For example, my father had a heart attack and I need to rush him to the emergency room so I will break the speed limit.
	Stage 6: Universal Ethical Principal Orientation Behaviors based on abstract ethical principles which take in multiple differing perspectives simultaneously.	Person acts to defend principals of equality, justice, equity. Personal conduct, intentions, character all play a role in decision making. Not everyone reaches this highest level.

Self-Efficacy

Self-efficacy reflects confidence in the ability to exert control over one's own motivation, behavior, and social environment. An example of students using self-efficacy would be working out a conflict on the playground without yelling or resorting to violence.

Self-Concept

Self-concept can be defined how children view their abilities. A child's self-concept begins to develop at birth. It also begins with how people interact with the child. As children grow, their ability to interact successfully with their environment nurtures a healthy self-concept. Teachers must nurture students' self-concept by modeling confidence and helping students navigate success and failure. Positive feedback when a student

Test Tip

In most questions on the exam that have to do with self-regulation and motivation, the teacher can help students by modeling the desired behavior and positively reinforcing that behavior. Want students to be kind? Model kind behavior. Want students to respect each other? Model that kind of behavior. Students do what the teacher does according to social learning theory. Modeling is often the correct answer on this exam.

does something desirable helps to build self-concept.

Self-Awareness

Self-awareness is the ability to see yourself clearly and objectively through reflection and introspection. Teachers of young children can help students become self-aware by talking through their feelings and helping them to self-reflect on their actions.

Self-Regulation

Self-regulation is the ability to monitor your own thoughts, emotions, and actions. Developmentally, school-aged children have not mastered self-regulation but are refining this skill on varying growth curves. Many students need scaffolded support to build self-regulation competencies in various learning settings. An example of this would be sitting quietly for story time even though the student wants to get up and play.

This page intentionally left blank.

B – Culture and Cultural Identity

1. Culture and interpersonal relationships

1. Culture and interpersonal relationships

Culture

Young learners explore concepts of likenesses and differences among cultural groups through social studies. Learners interact with class members and discover culturally based likenesses and differences. They begin to identify the cultural basis for some celebrations and ways of life in their community and in examples from across the world. It is important that teachers use culturally relevant materials and practices in the classroom.

Unity and Diversity

While diversity should be celebrated in the classroom and students should be given a chance to see how different cultures interact with each other, unity should also be stressed in the early childhood classroom.

An example of this might be to show how different cultures eat different foods or celebrate different holidays. Then the teacher makes connections to show students how similar different cultures are in terms of how they celebrate and how they interact with their families.

Test Tip

A big part of the social studies portion of the test is about showing students that we are more alike than different. Teachers do this by showing how cultures interact with family, food, and traditions.

Cultural Relevance

Classrooms are diverse places, and teachers must be culturally responsive when designing instruction and selecting materials to support instruction. Teachers must supplement with materials that acknowledge and celebrate different perspectives. These different cultural perspectives are integrated into the content areas, not just highlighted as special events. In other words, a culturally responsive approach means that teachers and students are celebrating and learning about diversity on a daily basis because it is an integral part of the classroom culture. This includes demonstrating sensitivity to various socioeconomic backgrounds and to individuals with disabilities (physical, cognitive, emotional, etc.).

When selecting supplementary materials, be careful to include:

- Literature/materials that reflect different cultures, especially those represented in the classroom
- Materials that show cultural diversity in educational settings (including post-secondary) and the workplace
- Multicultural celebrations
- Materials that celebrate history from various perspectives (race, nationality, gender, etc.)
- Articles or stories about overcoming socioeconomic barriers

Test Tip

When answering questions about cultural responsiveness in the classroom, be sure to select answer choices that reflect an ongoing approach to celebrating diversity. Celebrating Black History Month or Hispanic Heritage Month is beneficial to building a culturally responsive classroom. However, these happen one time per year. It's best to focus on everyday culturally responsive approaches, like continuously analyzing literature written by marginalized people or people from other cultures.

III. SOCIAL STUDIES

Multicultural classroom library

On the exam, you will be required to identify effective approaches to choosing multicultural texts and resources. When setting up a multicultural classroom library, a teacher should consider the following:

Accuracy. Accuracy of cultural representation is a crucial aspect of high-quality, multicultural literature, and books must contain current, correct information to avoid reinforcing stereotypes (Agosto, 2002; Shioshita, 1997).

Authentic dialogue. The dialogue in the text should accurately represent culturally specific oral traditions (Landt, 2006).

Presentation of information or issues. The information in the text should not leave out information that is unfavorable to the dominant culture. For example, a text about slavery should not have diluted information about the brutalities of slavery.

Tips on using a multicultural approach to selecting books and resources are:

- Avoid stereotypes and negative representations in print and illustrations.

- Ensure situations are realistic and positive.

- Confirm that the characters address conflicts and challenges and solve issues in a positive manner.

- Choose texts where diverse characters are the main characters with complex storylines.

Socio-economic considerations

Diversity is not always about the language students speak or the customs in which they participate. Diversity also applies to students' socio-economic circumstances. Some students will come to school without having eaten breakfast. Some students will come to school without basic necessities. It is the role of the teacher to provide effective instruction for these students. Assigning homework that requires computer and Internet access is not being considerate of students' socio-economic circumstances because some students do not have access to these tools at home. In addition, communicating with parents via email may not be most effective because parents may not have Internet access at home. Taking the time to consider all aspects of diversity in the classroom, including socioeconomic status, is essential in being an effective teacher.

Think about it!

One way teachers can support diversity in the classroom is by communicating effectively with parents. Because many families speak languages other than English, teachers must remember to send important information home in the native language. Also, not every student has access to the Internet or email. Therefore, providing a hard copy written in students' native languages is the most effective way to communicate upcoming events, classroom expectations, and other important information with families.

C – People, Places, and Environments

1. Spatial thinking, geographic perspectives, and the relationship between human beings and their environment

1. Spatial thinking, geographic perspectives, and the relationship between human beings and their environment

Geography is the study of the physical features of the Earth's surface and atmosphere, including how humans affect the physical features of the Earth and the ways these physical features affect humans (National Geographic, n.d.).

There are six essential elements of geography:

1. The world in spatial terms
2. Places and regions
3. Physical systems
4. Human systems
5. Environment and society
6. Uses of geography

This section focuses on world and regional geography which includes the world in spatial terms and places and regions. The other elements are discussed in the sections that follow.

World in spatial terms

The world in spatial terms refers to location on the Earth.

- **Absolute location**. Exact location of a point using latitude and longitude or an address. Example: 37N, 63W or "I live at 6570 Irish Rd."

- **Relative location**. Location of a point in relation to another point. Example: New York City is about 90 minutes from Philadelphia.

Quick Tip

Scenario: Ms. Jackson is telling students that the Rocky Mountains are west of the Mississippi River. She is giving them the **relative location** of the Rocky Mountains.

International Date Line. The International Date Line (IDL) is an imaginary line of navigation on the surface of the Earth that runs from the North Pole to the South Pole and indicates the change of one calendar day to the next. It passes through the middle of the Pacific Ocean, roughly following the 180° line of longitude, but deviates to pass around some territories and island groups. The IDL detours around political boundaries (Heim, 2018).

International Date Line

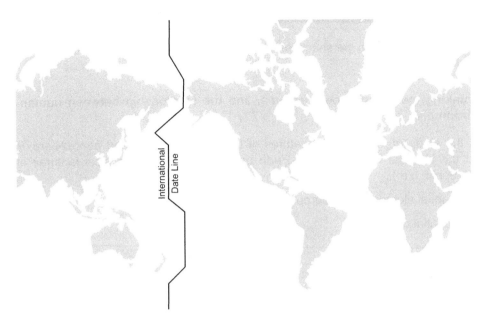

Hemispheres. The Earth is divided into four hemispheres: Northern, Southern, Eastern, and Western. The Equator divides the Earth into the Northern and Southern Hemispheres. The Prime Meridian (0° longitude) and the IDL divide the Earth into the Eastern and Western Hemispheres. The Eastern Hemisphere is east of the Prime Meridian and west of the IDL. The Western Hemisphere is west of the Prime Meridian and east of the IDL (National Geographic, n.d.).

According to an international agreement, the official Prime Meridian runs through Greenwich, England. Most of Asia and Africa are a part of the Eastern Hemisphere. The Americas and northwestern Africa are a part of the Western Hemisphere.

Equator and Prime Meridian

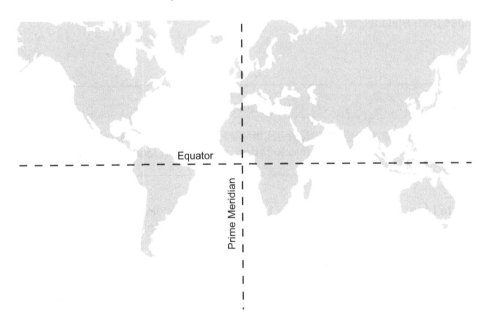

Geographic coordinate system is a series of gridlines used to describe the position on the Earth. It is made up of longitude and latitude lines.

Latitude and Longitude

Latitude and longitude are a system of lines used to describe the location of any place on Earth. Lines of latitude run in an east-west direction across Earth. Lines of longitude run in a north-south direction across Earth. Although these are only imaginary lines, they appear on maps and globes as if they actually existed.

Places and regions

Places are defined by both physical and human characteristics, including uses of the area.

Test Tip

If you were teaching students about time zones, you would use lines of longitude. You would show how time goes backwards when you move west across longitudinal lines.

Regions are areas broadly divided by physical characteristics, human impact characteristics, and the interaction of humanity and the environment. The Pacific Northwest, Southwest Florida, and the Sunbelt are all examples of regions.

- **Nation.** Nation refers to a community of people who share similar history, culture, and traditions and reside in the same area or territory (Merriam-Webster, 2019).

- **Sovereign state.** A sovereign state is a self-governing geopolitical entity that has defined borders and controls its internal sovereignty over its existence and affairs (Philpott, 2003).

- **Country.** A nation with its own government and economy that occupies a defined territory. A country may be an independent sovereign state or one that is occupied by another state (Merriam-Webster, 2019).

- **Continent.** A continent is one of the world's seven main continuous expanses of land. The seven continents are:

  1. Africa

  2. Antarctica

  3. Asia

  4. Australia

  5. Europe

  6. North America

  7. South America

Communities

A community is a group of people living in the same place or having a particular characteristic in common.

- **Urban Communities (city)** – those living in towns or cities with high population density.

- **Rural Communities (country)** – those living outside of towns or cities with low population density.

Geographic Features

Geographic Feature	Definition	Example
Archipelago	An archipelago is a group of islands or island chains	Hawaiian Islands
Atoll	A coral island that surrounds a lagoon	Maldives
Barrier island	A band of beach parallel to the mainland that protects the shore from the effects of the ocean	Clearwater Beach, Florida
Bays	An inlet of the sea or other body of water; usually smaller than a gulf	Chesapeake Bay, Ha Long Bay
Continent	Seven great divisions of land on the globe	Africa, North America
Deciduous forest	A forest of trees that lose their leaves seasonally	Eastern Deciduous Forrest, United States
Delta	A landform that forms from deposition of sediment carried by a river as the flow leaves its mouth and enters slower-moving or standing water	Mississippi Delta, Louisiana; Nile River Delta, Egypt
Desert	A barren area of landscape where little precipitation occurs and, consequently, living conditions are hostile for plant and animal life; can be hot or cold	Sahara, Antarctica
Fjord	A long, narrow, deep inlet of the sea between high cliffs	Skelton Inlet, Antarctica
Forest	A dense growth of trees and underbrush covering a large tract	Tongass National Forest, Alaska
Grassland	Land on which the natural dominant plant forms are grasses and herbs	North American prairies, Argentine pampas
Ice caps	A glacier forming on an extensive area of relatively level land and flowing outward from its center	Greenland Ice Sheet
Island	A tract of land surrounded by water and smaller than a continent	Ireland, Long Island
Isthmus	Narrow strip of land connecting two large land areas otherwise separated by bodies of water	Isthmus of Panama, connecting North and South America; Isthmus of Suez, connecting Africa and Asia
Mountain	A large area of raised land formed through tectonic movement or volcanic activity	Mt. St. Helens

Geographic Feature	Definition	Example
Mountain ranges	A series of mountains or mountain ridges closely related in position and direction	Andes, Rocky Mountains
Oceans	The whole body of saltwater that covers nearly three-fourths of the surface of Earth	Atlantic, Pacific
Peninsula	A land mass mostly surrounded by water and connected to a larger area of land	Florida
Plains	An extensive area of level or rolling, treeless country	The Great Plains
Plateaus	A usually extensive land area having a relatively level surface raised sharply above adjacent land on at least one side	Antarctic Plateau
Rain forest	A woodland with annual rainfall of 100 inches and heavy tree canopy	Amazon Rainforest, Daintree Rainforest
Rivers	A large system of natural flowing water	Amazon River
Seas	A body of saltwater that is partially enclosed by land	Baltic Sea, Mediterranean Sea
Taiga	A moist, subarctic forest of conifers that begins where the tundra ends	Alaska, Canada
Tundra	A level or rolling, treeless plain that is characteristic of arctic and subarctic regions, consists of black mucky soil with a permanently frozen subsoil, and has a dominant vegetation of mosses, lichens, herbs, and dwarf shrubs	Arctic tundra, alpine tundra
Valleys	An elongated depression of Earth's surface usually between ranges of hills or mountains	Yosemite Valley, Grand Canyon

Interdependence

Today's social, cultural, economic, and civic issues require students to apply knowledge, skills, and understanding as they address questions such as:

- Why do people decide to live where they do or move to other places?
- Why is location important?
- How do people interact with the environment and what are some of the consequences of those interactions?
- What physical and other characteristics lead to the creation of regions?
- How do maps, globes, geographic tools and geospatial technologies contribute to the understanding of people, places, and environments?

This page intentionally left blank.

D – Time, Continuity, and Change

1. Historical concepts and cronology

1. Historical concepts and cronology

Children in early grades learn to locate themselves in time and space and gain experience with sequencing to establish a sense of order and time. They start to understand the historical concepts in chronological order.

Using stories about history helps children develop understanding of ethical and moral issues. Children begin to recognize that stories can be told in different ways, and that individuals may hold divergent views about events in the past. They learn explain their views and why they are different. Importantly, they learn to support their claims with evidence from the text.

Chronological Thinking

Early childhood teachers must help students develop chronological thinking skills and help students distinguish between the past and present. Students should also be given the opportunities to develop their understanding of the future and how that is affected by the past. These skills begin by helping students use chronology in writing their own histories. Teachers can use a variety of tools to do this.

- **Timelines -** Timelines are graphic representations of the chronology of events in time. Timelines are used to display information in visual form. Students can also become actively engaged in learning the sequence of events in history by constructing timelines. For example, students can create a timeline of their lives or a timeline of a historical story to sequence events.

- **Maps –** Maps are fascinating to children. Teachers can use maps to help students understand special concepts. Students can also learn to make their own maps. For example, students can make maps of the classroom or playground. This introduces social studies concepts to young learners.

- **Graphs and Tables –** Reading and organizing data is an essential skill for early learners. Teachers must show students how to read graphs and tables but also how to use graphs and tables to organize data.

This page intentionally left blank.

E – Civics and Government

1. Importance of civic participation

1. Importance of civic participation

Civic participation is a big part of the early childhood social studies standards. The development of civic competence requires an understanding of the foundations of political thought, and the historical development of various structures of power, authority, and governance.

Learning the basic ideals and values of a constitutional democracy is crucial to understanding our system of government.

The United States is a republic, which means it is governed by elected representatives and by an elected leader (such as a president) rather than by a king or queen. The structure of the government and division of its power and the laws by which the nation is governed are outlined in the United States Constitution.

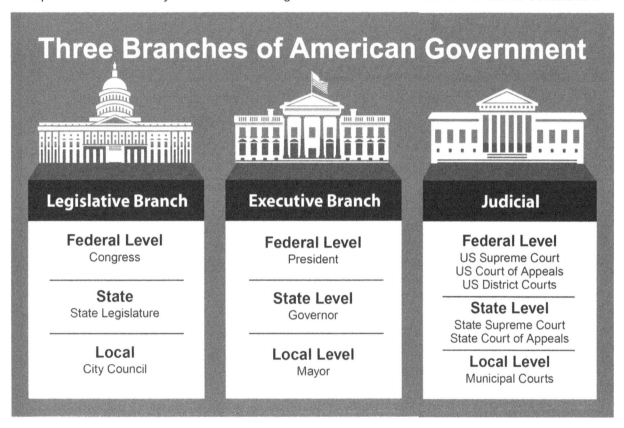

Federalism. Federalism refers to a type of government where powers are divided between the federal government and state governments.

States' rights. Political powers held for state governments rather than the federal government. The following fall under the umbrella of state powers:

- Issue licenses (e.g., marriage, drivers, business).
- Create local governments.
- Regulate industry.
- Ratify amendments to the State Constitution.
- Regulate commerce within state lines.

State government. State government is modeled after the federal government's three branches: executive, legislative, and judicial. Each state has its own constitution. State constitutions are much more detailed than their federal counterpart. (The White House, n.d.).

Local government. Local government is the public administration of towns, cities, counties, and districts. This type of government includes both county and municipal government structures. Citizens have much more contact with local governments than they do with the federal government (The White House, n.d.).

It is important to remember the roles and responsibilities citizens have as members of their community, state, nation, and the world.

U.S. Citizen Rights and Responsibilities

Quick Tip

Early childhood social studies teachers must help students understand government and how it affects their lives. There are many opportunities to do this in the early childhood classroom.

- Voting on activities to understand democracy
- Engaging in debates to express opinions
- Working in collaborative groups to solve problems.

Rights	Responsibilities
• Freedom to express yourself. • Freedom to worship as you wish. • Right to a prompt, fair trial by jury. • Right to vote in elections for public officials. • Right to apply for federal employment requiring U.S. citizenship. • Right to run for elected office. • Freedom to pursue "life, liberty, and the pursuit of happiness."	• Support and defend the Constitution. • Stay informed of the issues affecting your community. • Participate in the democratic process. • Respect and obey federal, state, and local laws. • Respect the rights, beliefs, and opinions of others. • Participate in your local community. • Pay income and other taxes honestly and on time to federal, state, and local authorities. • Serve on a jury when called upon. • Defend the country if the need should arise.

1. A 3rd grade teacher is using an interactive word wall with students for a sociology unit. The teacher asks 4 students to select 3 words related to the beliefs of a particular culture or people.

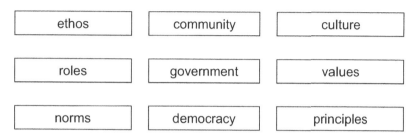

ethos	community	culture
roles	government	values
norms	democracy	principles

   Which student selected the correct group of words?

   A. **Jose**: norms, democracy, culture

   B. **Jessica**: roles, community, values

   C. **Samuel**: ethos, principles, values

   D. **Parker**: government, roles, norms

2. Which of the following is the most important lesson when teaching students about other cultures and heritages?

   A. Everyone should adhere to certain norms.

   B. People are more alike than different.

   C. Ancient civilizations contributed to modern society.

   D. The role of government most important in modern civilizations.

3. Which of the following activities would be most appropriate to show students how time zones work?

   A. In cooperative groups, have students read about time zones.

   B. Have students locate the equator on a map.

   C. Using a map, have students move figures east and west across lines of longitude.

   D. Using a map, have students move figures north and south across lines of latitude.

4. Which of the following is the most important reason to teach students media literacy in social studies class?

   A. To help students to be responsible with finances

   B. To help students to use the Internet

   C. To help students to work well in cooperative groups

   D. To help students discern reliable versus unreliable information

III. SOCIAL STUDIES

5. If the population in Country A continues as predicted, what will be the population in 2050?

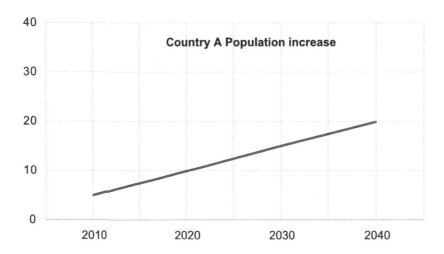

A. 20 million

B. 25 million

C. 30 million

D. 40 million

6. Students in a 1st grade classroom are sharing their tools during an activity. They also clean up after the activity is over, a task they have practiced several times before. They understand that when they work together to learn and then clean up, they will have a positive experience in the classroom. This is an example of:

A. Self-pacing

B. Self-esteem

C. Self-actualization

D. Self-efficacy

7. A prekindergarten teacher is working on a lesson about unity and how groups of people can work together to advance community needs while also helping individuals thrive. Which of the following scenarios below demonstrates this?

A. Families work together to grow a community garden so they can eat healthy foods.

B. A business builds new products to sell and uses the money to build more businesses in the area.

C. Every Tuesday, students in the community engage in a book club.

D. Students share their toys with each other during playtime.

8. Which of the following is the most effective activity to demonstrate democracy with prekindergarten students?

A. Have students work in cooperative groups to vote on classroom procedures.

B. Have students work together to complete tasks.

C. Show a video about how a bill is passed.

D. Have a guest speaker present important aspects of democracy.

9. Which of the following is an example of how humans can engage in positive citizenship?

    A. Finishing a task from beginning to end

    B. Working in cooperative groups to read complex text

    C. Listening to a friend express his or her feelings

    D. Volunteering to clean up the playground

10. Which of the following would be the best way to demonstrate the way humans impact the environment?

    A. Population growth

    B. Mortality rate

    C. Pollution

    D. Technology

Number	Answer	Explanation
1.	C	In this case, Samuel has chosen the correct 3 words. Ethos is a spirit or belief of a culture. Principles and values are also related to beliefs.
2.	B	This is a common theme in early childhood social science class. Understanding that people are more alike than different helps students to identify with others and embrace different cultures. This concept is mentioned several times in the test specifications for the exam.
3.	C	Time zones have to do with moving across lines of longitude. Time increases when you move east across lines of longitude. Time decreases when you move east across lines of longitude.
4.	D	Media literacy, especially in the social sciences, is essential in teaching students how to find reliable information. A big part of social studies in early childhood is to show students how to discern trustworthy information from unreliable information.
5.	B	The graph is increasing in increments of 5 million. Therefore, in year 2050, the population will be 25 million.
6.	D	Self-efficacy refers to a student's belief in his or her ability to execute behaviors necessary to produce specific performance attainments. Self-efficacy reflects confidence in the ability to exert control over one's own motivation, behavior, and social environment. The theorist Bandura is best known for his work with students' self-efficacy.
7.	A	The key here is for the group to not only work together, but to also help individuals thrive. Answer choice A is the only option that does that. The community garden helps the group, while also helping the individual thrive by creating the opportunity to eat healthy foods.
8.	A	Democracy is a form of government in which the people have the authority to choose their governing legislators. The best way to demonstrate this to students is by allowing them to form groups and vote on important classroom procedures. This choice is the most effective because it relates democracy to real life.
9.	D	Good citizenship is when a person fulfills a positive role and gives back to society. In early childhood, helping to clean up the playground is an example of good citizenship.
10.	C	Pollution is a direct result of human interaction with the environment.

IV. Science

This page intentionally left blank.

A – Fundamental Concepts and Processes of Scientific Inquiry

1. Fundamental concepts and processes of scientific inquiry in physical science, Earth and space science, life science, and engineering and technology

1. Fundamental concepts and processes of scientific inquiry in physical science, Earth and space science, life science, and engineering and technology

First things first—science is inquiry-based, meaning students must be given the opportunity to interact with the concepts they are studying. For example, talking about living and nonliving things is one thing. However, going outside and observing living and nonliving things is quite another. Students must have the opportunity to touch, observe, and interact with the environment they are studying.

According to the National Science Teacher Association (NSTA), effective science instruction includes:

- Having pedagogical knowledge.
- Providing learning opportunities that meet the individual needs of students.
- Placing the learner at the center of instruction.
- Facilitating learning opportunities that develop students' conceptual understanding.

Teachers must know the science content, empower the students to learn, differentiate to meet the needs of diverse population, and foster inquiry-based learning activities. Students must touch, feel, and observe to understand science.

There are two primary types of learning experiences. The first is a **formal learning experience**, which is generally teacher-led and occurs in a classroom or lab. The second is an **informal learning experience**, which can take place anywhere outside of a formal learning environment and are often collaborative or self-directed.

Think about it!

If the teacher wants her students to understand the diet of an owl, she should give them an opportunity to dissect owl pellets (a mass of undigested parts of a bird's food that some bird species occasionally regurgitate). Reading about owl diets is ok, but dissecting owl pellets is much better.

Characteristics of Formal and Informal Learning

Formal	Informal
Compulsory	Voluntary
Structured	Unstructured
Assessed	Non-assessed
Evaluated	Unevaluated
Sequenced	Open-ended
Have classroom context	Out-of-school context
Are curriculum-based	Non-curriculum-based
Have fewer unintended outcomes	Have many unintended outcomes
Teacher-directed	Non-directed or learner-directed
Feature solitary work	Feature social intercourse
Have empirically-measured outcomes	Have less directly measurable outcomes

Integrating both formal and informal experiences strengthens overall learning. Students who can informally apply and explore the lessons they learn in a formal environment consistently outperform students who cannot do this.

Unifying processes of science

There are five main ideas under the unifying concepts and processes of science.

Main Idea	Science Example
1. Systems, order, and organizations	Parts are related to the whole. For example, the atmosphere affects the entire climate of Earth. That climate impacts humans. Humans impact the environment.
2. Evidence, models, and explanations	Students use a model of the solar system to discuss the relationship among planets and the sun.
3. Change, constancy, and measurement	Because of Earth's tilt on its axis, we experience changes in seasons as the we move through the year.
4. Evolution and equilibrium	Phases of matter and changes in Earth's sky are examples of evolution and equilibrium.
5. Form and function	Earth's features like its mass and shape impact functions such as gravity and rotation.

IV. SCIENCE

The Study of Science

Science is dynamic, and what is true one day may not be true the next. Scientists use a variety of mechanisms to describe, test, and validate phenomena.

- **Hypothesis.** An idea that may contribute important new knowledge for the evaluation of a scientific theory.

- **Models.** Used to communicate ideas and to represent abstract phenomena. For example, the solar system is impossible to see in a classroom or lab; however, a model of the solar system is easily accessible in a classroom or lab.

- **Theories.** Based on a body of evidence and many experiments, trials, and tests. Theories are explanations for observable phenomena. Scientific theories are based on a body of evidence developed over time.

- **Scientific explanations.** Describe the mechanisms for natural events.

- **Scientific laws.** Regularities or mathematical descriptions of natural phenomena.

- **Durability.** The ability to hold up over time. For example, the law of gravity is durable. It has held up over time.

- **Tentativeness.** Willingness to modify ideas as new evidence is presented. Science is dynamic and what is true one day may not be true the next. Tentative means uncertain, which is an asset in science. When students are uncertain, they conduct experiments using the scientific method to figure it out.

- **Replication.** Getting the same result when an experiment is repeated.

- **Reliance on evidence.** Using concepts from the text, studies, and research to support opinions or claims. It is important to teach students to rely on data and evidence when making claims. It is also important to reference this evidence when communicating ideas and findings in science.

Scientific method

The scientific method is a body of techniques for investigating phenomena, acquiring new knowledge, or correcting and integrating previous knowledge. To be termed scientific, a method of inquiry is commonly based on empirical or measurable evidence subject to specific principles of reasoning.

Students in science:

- **Observe**. Employ the five senses to interact with phenomena and recording findings.

- **Classify.** Arrange living and nonliving things based on attributes.

- **Predict**. Make assumptions based on evidence.

- **Hypothesize**. State a prediction based on evidence.

- **Investigate**. Conduct experiments.

Test Tip

Steps to the scientific method

1. Make an observation.

2. Ask a question.

3. Form a hypothesis.

4. Conduct an experiment.

5. Analyze the data and draw a conclusion

6. Replicate

This page intentionally left blank.

B – Physical Science

1. The physical world

   - States of matter
   - Forms of energy
   - Position and motion of objects

1. The physical world

Physical and chemical properties and structure of matter

- **Solid.** Particles are very close together.
- **Liquid.** Particles are closer together than a gas but farther apart than a solid.
- **Gas.** Particles are very far apart.

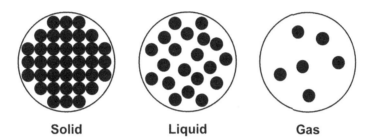

| Solid | Liquid | Gas |

- **Texture.** Characteristics and appearance of an object given by the size, shape, density, arrangement, proportion of its elementary parts. Examples of texture include hard, soft, rough, smooth, coarse, fine, matt, glossy.
- **Hardness.** A measure of how much a material resists changes in shape. For example, hard things resist pressure. Some examples of hard materials are diamond, steel, ice, granite, concrete.
- **Freezing point.** The temperature at which a liquid changes to a solid
- **Melting point.** The temperature at which a solid changes to a liquid.
- **Boiling Point.** The temperature at which a liquid changes into a gas.

Mass

Mass is how much matter there is in an object. Mass does not equal weight. For example, Jupiter, a planet made of gas, is much denser than Earth, a planet made of rock.

$$mass = density \times volume$$

Volume

Volume is the amount of space an object takes up.

$$volume = \frac{mass}{density}$$

Changes in Matter

Physical changes result in a change in **shape** and **size**. Chemical changes result in a change that forms a **new substance** at the **molecular level**.

Changes in Matter

Physical		Chemical
Tearing		Rotting
Folding		Burning
Melting		Cooking
Freezing		Rusting
Evaporating		
Cutting		

Phase Changes in Matter

Changes in matter can happen by removing or adding energy in the form of boiling, condensation, and evaporation.

1. **Boiling.** Rapid vaporization of a liquid (liquid to gas).

2. **Condensation.** Water that collects as droplets on a cold surface when humid air is in contact with it (gas to liquid).

3. **Evaporation.** Vaporization of a liquid that occurs from the surface of a liquid into a gaseous phase (liquid to gas).

Quick Tip

Have you ever walked into a grocery store after your workout, and you become chilly? That's because when water evaporates, it leaves behind cooler air. It's called *temperature moderation*, and it's the amazing property of water a property that is essential for life on Earth.

Mixtures

A mixture is a material system made up of two or more different substances that are mixed but are not combined chemically. The identities of the mixed elements are retained in a mixture. There are two types of mixtures: **homogeneous** and **heterogeneous**.

Homogeneous Mixture	Heterogeneous Mixture	Colloid	Suspension	Solutions
homo = same	hetero = different	homogeneous mixture	heterogeneous mixture	homogeneous mixture
You cannot see different parts of the mixture.	You can see different parts of the mixture.	One substance of microscopically dispersed insoluble particles is suspended throughout another substance. Particles do not settle and cannot be separated out by ordinary filtering.	Contains solid particles that are sufficiently large for sedimentation.	The dissolving agent is the solvent.
coffee, creamy peanut butter, Kool-Aid	chicken noodle soup, cereal	gels, emulsions	orange juice, salad dressing	salt water, sugar water

Atoms

- **Atoms.** The smallest part of an element that retains its chemical properties. More than 99.94% of an atom's mass is in the nucleus.
- **Electrons.** Negatively charged subatomic particles that circle around the atom's nucleus.
- **Neutrons.** Neutrally charged subatomic particles that are located in the atom's nucleus.
- **Protons.** Positively charged subatomic particles that are located in the atom's nucleus.

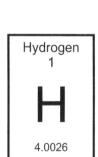

Elements

- **Elements.** More than 100 substances that cannot be chemically interconverted or broken down into simpler substances and are primary constituents of matter.
- **Atomic number.** How an element is identified. It is also the number of protons in the nuclei of its atoms.
- **Periodic table of elements.** A tabular display of chemical elements arranged by atomic number and characteristics.

Hydrogen
1
H
4.0026

IV. SCIENCE

The Periodic Table of the Elements

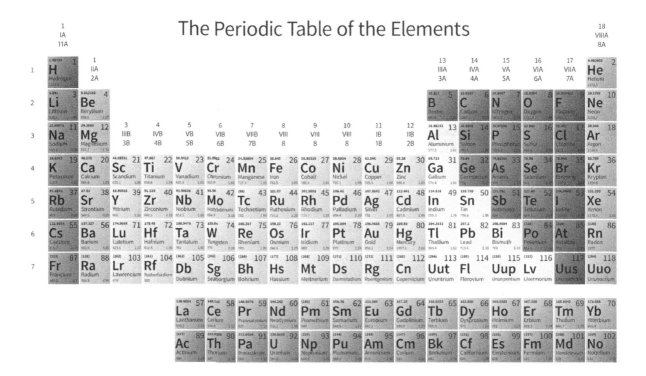

The periodic table can be used a variety of ways and is broken up several ways.

- **Groups**. Vertical/columns
- **Periods**. Horizontal/rows
- **Metals**. Shiny, good conductors of electricity
- **Nonmetals**. Dull, poor conductors of electricity
- **Metalloids**. Dull or shiny, good semiconductors
- **Noble gases**. Last column on the right of the periodic table

Energy

Energy is a property that can be transferred in between and among objects. Energy can also be converted into different forms.

Kinetic energy. Object is in motion; the actual movement of an object. For example, a rock rolling down a hill or a swing swinging in the air both have kinetic energy. Because the objects are in motion, they have kinetic energy.

Potential energy. The energy possessed by an object or individual by virtue of its position relative to others, stresses within itself, electric charge, and other factors. For example, a rock on the top of the hill has potential to roll down; therefore, the rock has potential energy. A swing being pulled to the top before it is released has potential energy.

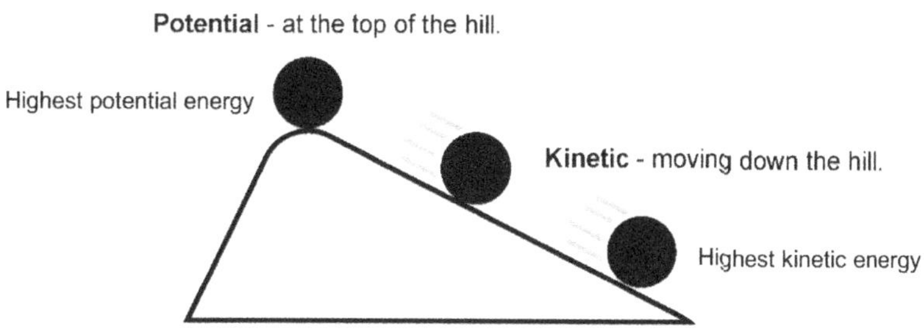
Potential - at the top of the hill.
Highest potential energy
Kinetic - moving down the hill.
Highest kinetic energy

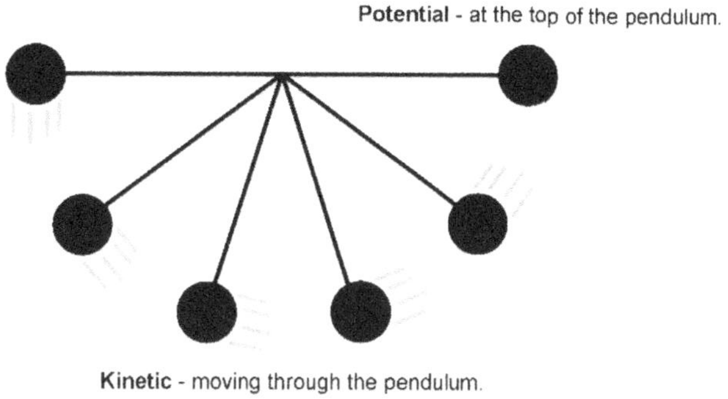
Potential - at the top of the pendulum.
Kinetic - moving through the pendulum.

On this exam, you will be required to differentiate among different forms of energy when answering questions.

A **force** is any interaction that, when unopposed, will change the motion of an object. A force can cause an object with mass to change its velocity (including beginning motion from a state of rest).

Friction is the force resisting the relative motion of solid surfaces, fluid layers, and material elements sliding against each other.

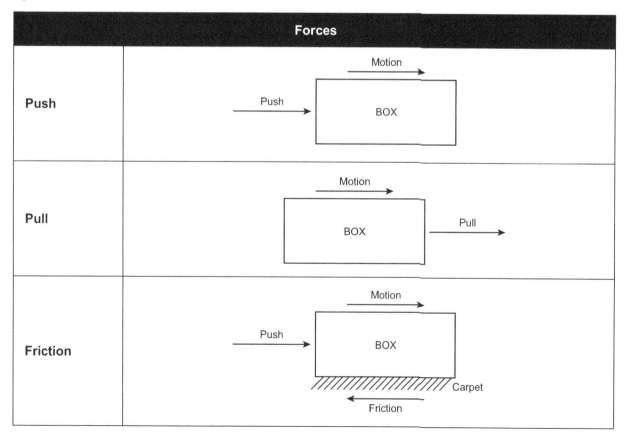

Forces	
Push	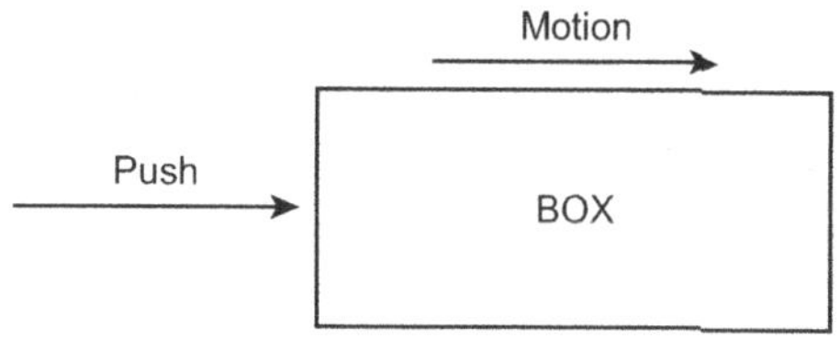Motion Push BOX
Pull	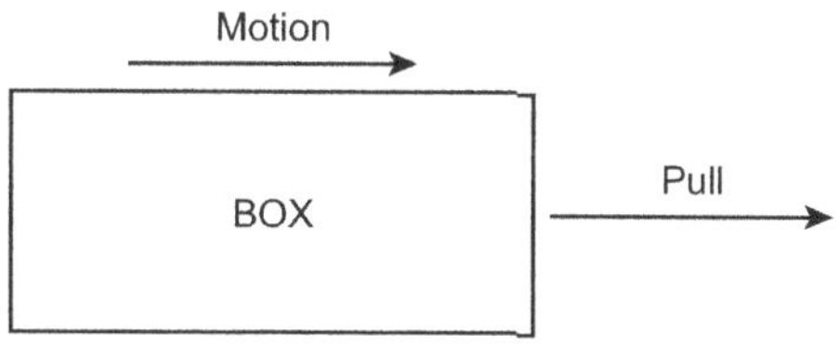Motion BOX Pull
Friction	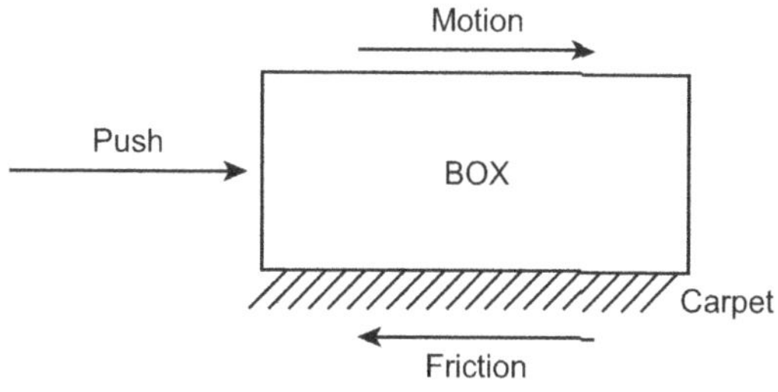Motion Push BOX Carpet Friction

Forms of Energy

Form	What It Does...	Examples
Mechanical	Objects in motion	Swing
Electrical	The movement of electrons through a wire	Light bulb
Chemical	Rearrangement of molecular structure	Photosynthesis, lighting a match, rusting
Thermal/heat	The movement of particles because of heat and friction.	Boiling water
Sound	The movement of energy through a substance, such as air or water, in the form of waves.	Sonic boom
Light	Electromagnetic radiation where photons are produced when an object's atoms heat up.	Fire

Test Tip

On the early childhood science subtest, you will probably encounter questions about sound waves versus other types of waves (light and heat). Remember, sound waves must travel through a medium (solid, liquid or gas); they cannot travel in a vacuum like light and heat waves can. That's why there is light and heat in space, but there is no sound in space.

Heat transfer

Heat transfer is the exchange of thermal energy between physical systems.

- **Convection.** The transfer of heat by the actual movement of the warmed matter. For example, in a convection oven, air is moved by a fan around the food.

- **Conduction.** The transfer of heat from particle to particle. For example, if a cold spoon is placed in hot soup, the spoon will get hotter until the soup and the spoon become the same temperature.

- **Radiation.** The transfer of heat from electromagnetic waves through space. Sunlight is a form of radiation.

Convection

In a convection oven, a fan swirls heat around the food.

Conduction

The spoon handle will get hot because it is touching the hot water

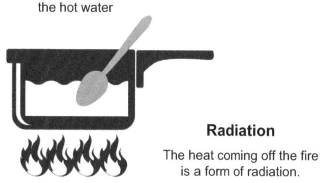

Radiation

The heat coming off the fire is a form of radiation.

Quick Tip

We use wooden spoons when cooking because wood is a bad conductor of heat. The handle of a wooden spoon stays cool even when submerged in hot water. A metal spoon will eventually become as hot as the water because metal is a good conductor of heat.

Electricity

Electricity can be defined as the flow of an electric charge. The most familiar electricity is the type used in homes and businesses to power lights and appliances. Electrical circuits allow electricity to flow in a loop and power different things.

Quick Tip

When a circuit is open, the loop is not closed; therefore, the light will not turn on. Only when the circuit is closed can the electricity travel around the loop fully and light the bulb.

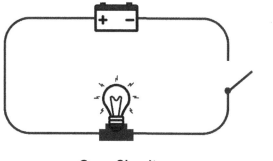

Open Circuit

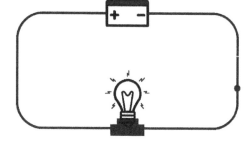

Closed Circuit

Types of circuits

Series circuits. The components are arranged end to end. The electric current flows through the first component, then through the next component, and so on until it reaches the battery again.

Parallel circuits. A circuit with branches that allows multiple applications to happen at once.

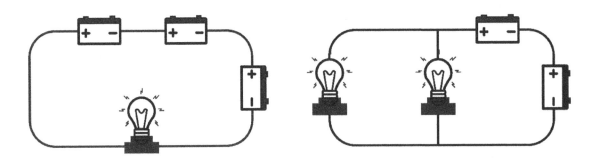

| Series Circuits | Parallel Circuits |

Conductors and Insulators

Conductors (good for electricity)	Insulators (bad for electricity)
Wire	Rubber
Metal	Cloth
Water	Polystyrene (Styrofoam)

Lightning

Lightning is a giant spark of electricity in the atmosphere between clouds, the air, or the ground. As lightning starts, air acts as an insulator between the positive and negative charges in the cloud and between the cloud and the ground. When the opposite charges build up enough, this insulating capacity of the air breaks down, and there is a rapid discharge of electricity (NSSL, 2019).

Cloud-to-ground lightning occurs between opposite charges within the thunderstorm cloud (intra-cloud lightning) or between opposite charges in the cloud and on the ground (cloud-to-ground lightning).

Quick Tip

Right before cloud-to-ground lightning occurs, the the ground becomes positively charged because negative charges seep into the earth leaving fewer electrons on the earth's surface. The negative charges in the cloud are attracted to the positive charges on the earth's surface. Therefore, the negative charges move down the cloud close to the earth's surface. When the attraction is strong enough, lightning occurs.

Magnetism

Magnetism is the force exerted by magnets when they attract or repel each other. Magnetism is caused by the motion of electric charges (National Geographic, n.d.).

Opposite poles attract – N & S

Same poles repel – S & S and N & N

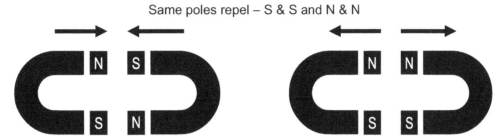

Newton's Laws of Motion

1. An object either remains at rest or continues to move at a constant velocity unless acted upon by a force.

2. Force is equal to the change in motion (mV) per change in time. For a constant mass, force equals mass times acceleration .

3. For every action, there is an equal and opposite reaction.

(NASA, n.d.)

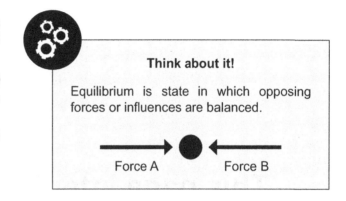

Think about it!

Equilibrium is state in which opposing forces or influences are balanced.

Force A   Force B

IV. SCIENCE

This page intentionally left blank.

C – Earth and Space Science

1. Earth and space

   • Sun, Moon and stars

   • Changes on Earth

   • Properties of Earth's materials

1. Earth and space

Earth is the third planet from the sun. Earth is the densest planet in the solar system, the largest of the solar system's four terrestrial planets, and the only astronomical object known to harbor life.

The Sun is the star at the center of the solar system. It is the most important source of energy for life on Earth.

The Moon is Earth's only natural satellite. The moon is thought to have formed approximately 4.5 billion years ago, not long after Earth.

Earth's tilt

Seasons are a result of Earth's **tilt on its axis.** When Earth is tilted toward the sun, it is warmer (summer). When Earth is tilted away from the sun, it is colder (winter). During spring and fall, Earth is tilted on its side. See diagram below.

Quick Tip

The sun is a star. The reason the sun appears so large is that it is the closest star to Earth.

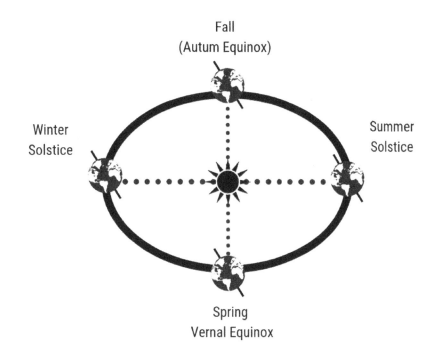

Season	Description
Fall – Autumn Equinox	Date in the fall when Earth experiences 12 hours of daylight and 12 hours of darkness. This occurs around September 23.
Summer – Solstice	Earth's maximum tilt is toward the sun, causing the longest period of daylight. This occurs around June 22.
Spring – Vernal Equinox	Date in the spring when Earth experiences 12 hours of daylight and 12 hours of darkness. This occurs around March 21.
Winter – Solstice	The North Pole is tilted furthest away from the sun, causing the shortest period of daylight. This occurs around December 21.

Heliocentric and geocentric

The Scientific Revolution began as the Renaissance was coming to an end. The Scientific Revolution marked the emergence of modern science and the heliocentric model regarding the universe. The heliocentric theory, introduced by Nicolaus Copernicus, positioned the sun at the center of the universe. Copernicus also asserted Earth rotates on its axis while revolving around the sun. Up until that point, it was believed Earth sat stationary at the center of the universe (the geocentric theory). In his book, On the Revolutions of Heavenly Spheres, Copernicus' heliocentric model replaced the geocentric model.

The Moon

The moon affects the tides. When the part of the moon that is illuminated is increasing, the moon phase is waxing. When the part of the moon that is illuminated is decreasing, the moon phase is waning. A waxing moon is illuminated on the right side; a waning moon is illuminated on the left side.

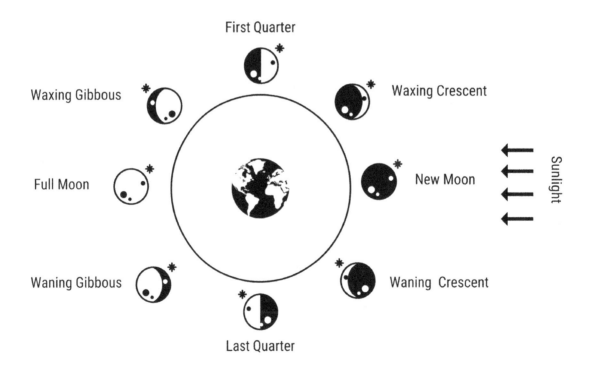

Stars

A star is a luminous ball of gas, mostly hydrogen and helium, held together by its own gravity. A star's color relies on its temperature—hotter stars emit bluer light, and cooler stars emit redder light (Temming 2014).

Type	Color	Temperature
O	Blue	Over 25,000 Kelvin
B	Blue	11,000–20,000 Kelvin
A	Blue	7,500–11,000 Kelvin
F	Blue to White	6,000–7,500 Kelvin
G	White to Yellow	5,000–6,000 Kelvin
K	Orange to Red	3,500–5,000 Kelvin
M	Red	Under 3,500 Kelvin

Lunar eclipse positions

A **lunar eclipse** occurs when the moon passes directly behind Earth into its umbra (shadow).

Moon

Earth

Sun

IV. SCIENCE

Solar eclipse positions

A **solar eclipse** happens when the moon moves in front of the sun.

Earth

Moon

Sun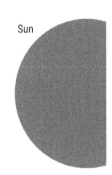

Earth's patterns, cycles, and change

Earth goes through several patterns, cycles, and changes.

- **Patterns**. Earth spins on its axis. It makes one full rotation on its axis every 24 hours. Earth also revolves around the sun. It takes 365 days for Earth to make one full revolution around the sun.

- **Cycles**. Earth's rotation on its axis and revolution around the sun causes cycles on Earth: day, night, seasons, weather. Other cycles include the phases of the moon, water cycle, and life cycles (covered in Category 2 – Life Sciences).

- **Changes**. Earth goes through various changes. Some changes happen quickly; for example, an earthquake or a storm can change Earth rapidly. Other changes happen slowly; for example, the North American and Eurasian tectonic plates are separated by the Mid-Atlantic Ridge. The two continents are moving away from each other at the rate of about 2.5 centimeters (1 inch) per year (National Geographic, n.d.).

Quick Tip

Continental Drift was first proposed by Alfred Wegener, continental drift suggests the Earth's continents were all once one big landmass and over time, separated or drifted apart because of plate tectonics.

The Earth's plates are still constantly moving. Plate tectonics cause earthquakes, volcanic eruptions, and rift valleys.

Earth's magnetic poles

Earth has a magnetic field that extends from its interior to outer space. A compass is calibrated based on Earth's magnetic field. Over time, Earth's poles reverse—every 200,000 to 300,000 years. Magnetic fields morph, push, and pull at one another, with multiple poles emerging at odd latitudes throughout the process. Scientists estimate reversals have happened at least hundreds of times over the past 3 billion years.

On Earth, the magnetic field S pole is near Earth's geographic North Pole. The magnetic field N pole is near Earth's geographic South Pole. This makes a compass usable for navigation.

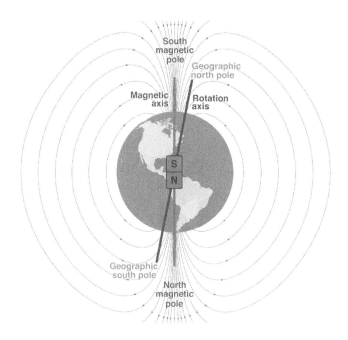

Solar system

The solar system is a planetary system that orbits the sun. The solar system consists of the sun and everything that orbits around it. This includes the eight planets and their natural satellites (such as our moon), dwarf planets and their satellites, as well as asteroids, comets, and countless particles of smaller debris (NASA, n.d.).

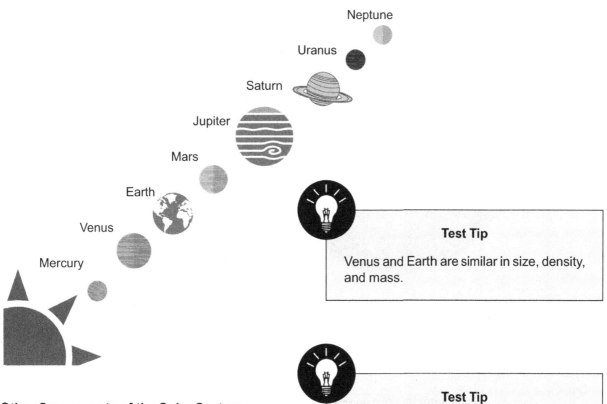

Test Tip

Venus and Earth are similar in size, density, and mass.

Test Tip

Understand the comparison of Mars and Earth. Mars is like Earth in terms of rotation and tilt on its axis. A Martian day is just over 24 hours, and its rotation axis is tilted by about the same amount as Earth's rotation axis.

Other Components of the Solar System

- **Comets** – A chunk of ice and rock originating outside of the solar system.
- **Asteroids** – A chunk of rock and metal in orbit in between Mars and Jupiter.
- **Meteorite** – A small asteroid.

Quick Tip

Light Year

A light year is a unit of astronomical distance equal to the distance light travels in one year. For example, if an event occurs 13 light years away, it will take 13 years to observe the event from Earth.

Speed of Light

The speed of light in a vacuum is approximately 300,000 km/sec. In a vacuum is where speed of light is fastest. Traveling through any other medium, the speed of light is slower.

Solid Earth

Earth is made up of several layers: crust/lithosphere, mantle, and core.

Earth gets denser toward the center.

The temperature increases deeper into Earth. For example, the mantle is 1900°K, the outer core is 3000°K, and the inner ore is 5000—7000°K.

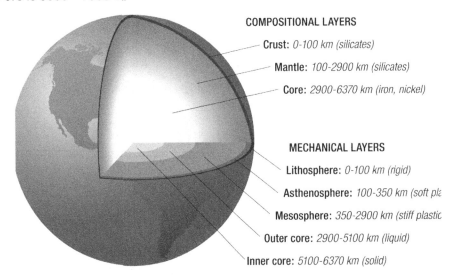

COMPOSITIONAL LAYERS

Crust: *0-100 km (silicates)*

Mantle: *100-2900 km (silicates)*

Core: *2900-6370 km (iron, nickel)*

MECHANICAL LAYERS

Lithosphere: *0-100 km (rigid)*

Asthenosphere: *100-350 km (soft pla*

Mesosphere: *350-2900 km (stiff plastic*

Outer core: *2900-5100 km (liquid)*

Inner core: *5100-6370 km (solid)*

Composition Layers		
Layer	**Definition**	**Depth**
Crust (Lithosphere)	The outermost solid layer of Earth.	0 – 100 km
Mantle	The mantle is not liquid; it is ductile or plastic, which means that some parts of the mantle can flow under certain conditions and changes in pressure. The mantle is mainly composed of aluminum and silicates.	100 – 900 km
Core	The innermost layers of Earth. Earth has an outer core (liquid) and an inner core (solid). The core is mainly composed of nickel and iron.	2900 – 6370 km

Earth's atmosphere is a layer of gases surrounding the planet. The gases present in Earth's atmosphere are:

- **Nitrogen:** 78%
- **Oxygen:** 21%
- **Argon:** 0.09%
- **Carbon dioxide:** 0.01%
- **Helium:** small traces
- **Neon:** small traces
- **Other gases:** small traces

Quick Tip

Nitrogen and oxygen make up 99% of the gases in Earth's atmosphere, with nitrogen being the most prevalent.

Researchers assert Earth's atmosphere was formed from volcanic eruptions that happened early in Earth's history.

Earth's 5 Spheres – Above the Crust

Earth is made up of different types of spheres.

- **Lithosphere** – The outermost shell of Earth. Earth's crust is the lithosphere.

- **Hydrosphere** – All the water on Earth in liquid form. For example, lakes, rivers, and oceans are all part of the hydrosphere.

- **Biosphere** – The global sum of all ecosystems and living organisms.

- **Cryosphere** – The masses of frozen water. For example, frozen lakes, frozen rivers, frozen oceans, and glaciers are part of the cryosphere.

- **Atmosphere** – The layer of gases that surround the plane.

Quick Tip

Glaciers contain 69% of Earth's fresh water. Ice and glaciers are part of the water cycle.

The Water Cycle

The water cycle, also called the hydrologic cycle, is a continuous circulation of water throughout Earth and Earth's atmosphere.

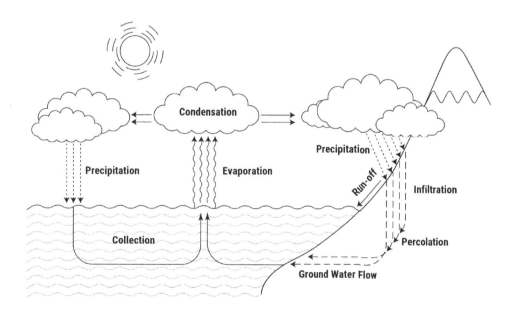

- **Precipitation** is rain and snow.

- **Evaporation** is when water turns from a liquid to a gas (water vapor).

- **Condensation** is when water vapor turns back into liquid—water collects as droplets on a cold surface when humid air is in contact with it, forming clouds.

- **Transpiration** is when plants suck water from roots to the small pores in leaves, releasing the water vapor into the atmosphere.

Test Tip

Be sure you know the main stages of the water cycle

- Evaporation
- Condensation
- Precipitation
- Transpiration

Earth's atmosphere also contains multiple layers:

- **Troposphere**: 0–12 km above Earth. *Most of Earth's weather occurs here.

- **Stratosphere**: 12–50 km above Earth. *Contains the ozone layer.

- **Mesosphere**: 50–80 km above Earth.

- **Thermosphere**: 80–700 km above Earth.

- **Exosphere**: 700–1000 km above Earth.

The ozone layer absorbs 97 – 99% of the sun's ultraviolet light and is contained in the stratosphere. This layer contains high levels of ozone (O_3). Two decades of scientific research has shown that human-produced chemicals are responsible for the observed depletions of the ozone layer. (NOAA, n.d.).

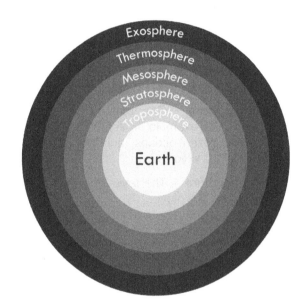

Quick Tip

When we drive cars, carbon dioxide (CO_2) is released into the atmosphere. The CO_2 is trapped inside the ozone layer and prevents the sun's rays from escaping, which contributes to Earth's increase in temperature.

Energy resources play a critical role in everyday human life. We use energy to power everything from a coffee machine to the space shuttle. Our energy resources come from the Earth in a variety of forms. Some energy resources cannot be renewed as quickly as they are being consumed (nonrenewable); some energy resources can be renewed quickly by the Earth's physical processes (renewable).

- **Clean energy**. Energy from wind, solar, wind, water, geothermal, biomass, and nuclear

- **Fossil energy**. Energy from coal, oil, and natural gas

- **Electric power**. Energy from charged particles

Renewable and Nonrenewable Resources

Renewable	Nonrenewable
Solar	Fossil fuels
Wind	Coal
Hydro power	Natural gas

Earth's materials

A rock is any naturally occurring solid mass or aggregate of minerals or mineraloid matter. Rocks are categorized by the minerals they include, their chemical composition, and their formation (origin). Rocks are usually grouped into three main categories: igneous, metamorphic and sedimentary. Rocks form the Earth's outer solid layer: the lithosphere.

Types of Rocks

Type	Igneous	Metamorphic	Sedimentary
Made from...	lava, magma	heat pressure	deposition, cementation
Looks like...	glassy, smooth surface, gas bubble holes, random arrangement of minerals	sparkly crystals, ribbon-like layers	sand grains or visible pebbles; fossils may be visible
Examples	granite, pumice, obsidian	marble, slate, gneiss	conglomerate, sandstone, limestone, shale

Soil

Soil is a mixture of minerals, organic matter, gases, liquids, and many organisms that together support life on Earth.

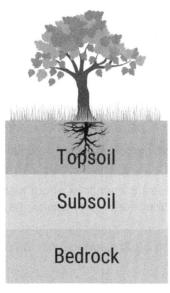

Topsoil

Subsoil

Bedrock

Quick Tip

Aquifers are bodies of permeable rock which can contain or transmit ground water. Bedrock often makes a good aquifer.

IV. SCIENCE

Processes of the lithosphere (crust)

Geologic formations are formations made from rocks that exist on the lithosphere. Examples include volcanoes, mountains, and canyons.

Mountains are formed as a result of Earth's tectonic plates smashing together.

Volcanoes are formed when magma from within Earth's upper mantle erupts through the surface.

Canyons are formed by weathering and erosion caused by the movement of rivers. Canyons are also formed by tectonic activity.

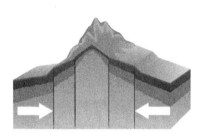  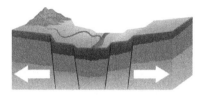

Earthquakes

Earthquakes are usually caused when plates rub against each other in an opposite motion, and rock underground suddenly breaks along a fault. This sudden release of energy causes seismic waves that make the ground shake.

Scientists assign a magnitude rating to earthquakes based on the strength and duration of their seismic waves. A quake measuring 3 to 4.9 is considered minor or light; 5 to 6.9 is moderate to strong; 7 to 7.9 is major; and 8 or more is great.

Test Tip

For the exam it is helpful to remember the Ring of Fire, which is a ring of volcanoes around the outer edge of the Pacific Ocean. These volcanoes are a result of subduction of oceanic plates beneath lighter continental plates. In fact, most of Earth's volcanoes and earthquakes happen along the Ring of Fire. (National Geographic, n.d.).

Seismic waves

A seismic wave is an elastic wave caused by an earthquake. There are three types of seismic waves:

1. **Primary (P waves).** These are the fastest waves (5 kilometers per second or approximately 3 miles per second) and can travel through solid, liquids, and gases.

2. **Secondary (S waves).** Secondary waves travel through Earth's interior at about half the speed of primary waves. Secondary waves can travel through rock, but unlike primary waves, they cannot travel through liquids or gases.

3. **Surface.** Surface waves are seismic waves that move along Earth's surface, not through its interior. Surface waves are the slowest of the three seismic waves.

Tsunamis

Tsunamis are giant waves caused by earthquakes or volcanic eruptions under the sea. Out in the depths of the ocean, tsunami waves do not dramatically increase in height. However, as the waves travel inland, they build up to higher and higher heights as the depth of the ocean decreases. The speed of tsunami waves depends on ocean depth. Tsunamis may travel as fast as jet planes over deep waters, only slowing down when they reach shallow waters (NOAA, 2019).

Plate tectonics is the theory that Earth's outer shell is divided into several plates that glide over the mantle or the rocky inner layer above the core. The plates move and separate, causing Earth to separate and change.

Divergent – Pulling apart   **Convergent** – Coming together   **Subduction** – Sideways and downward movement of the edge of a plate into the mantle beneath another plate

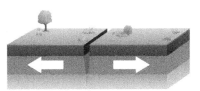

This page intentionally left blank.

D – Life Science

1. Living organisms and natural systems

   - Organisms and their environments

   - The life cycles of organisms including heredity

   - Ecosystems and organism interdependence

1. Living organisms and natural systems

Living things have characteristics like being physical entities and experiencing biological processes. Examples of these include homeostasis, cell division, cellular respiration, and photosynthesis. Nonliving things do not have these processes and are classified as **inanimate**.

Example question

Which of the following best describes a characteristic of a nonliving object?

   A. Photosynthesis

   B. Inanimation

   C. Respiration

   D. Homeostasis

Correct answer: B

Nonliving things cannot experience photosynthesis, respiration, or homeostasis—these are all characteristics of living things. Nonliving things are classified as inanimate.

Test Tip

Living things respond to stimuli like light and temperature. Non-living things do not respond to stimuli. Remember that for the exam.

Cell theory is made up of three components:

1. All living things are composed of cells.

2. The cell is the smallest unit of life.

3. All cells come from pre-existing cells.

The structural hierarchy of life is as follows:

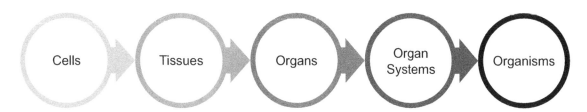

Cells → Tissues → Organs → Organ Systems → Organisms

IV. SCIENCE

Animal and plant cell structures

Animal and plant cells are both eukaryotic in structure. However, there are functional differences between an animal cell and a plant cell.

Animal cell

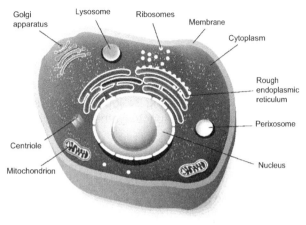

Plant cell

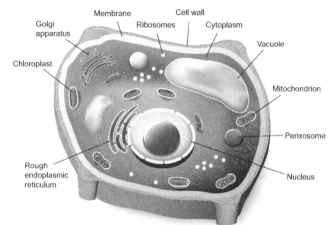

Plant Cells	Animal Cells
Cell wall	Plasma membrane
Chloroplast	No chloroplast
Photosynthesis (CO_2 + H_2O + light = Carbohydrates)	Cellular respiration (Carbohydrates + O_2 = CO_2 and H_2O

Classification

The **classification of living things** was first done by Carl Linnaeus, as set forth in his Systema Naturae (1735). His system classifies all living things into major groups according to physical features, behaviors, and development.

Domains. Archaea and Bacteria consist exclusively of prokaryotic microorganisms. All other plant and animal life are part of the Eukarya domain.

Kingdoms. There are six kingdoms that broadly divide life into classifications, such as plants and animals.

Phylum. A division based on physical characteristics, such as vertebrates and invertebrates.

Taxonomy of Linnaeus

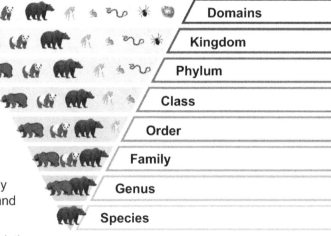

Class. A classification based primarily on physical features. In the animal kingdom, for example, this is where mammals are separated from reptiles and birds.

Order. A subdivision where animals can be divided based on behavioral characteristics, such as whether they are carnivores or herbivores. In the plant kingdom, this is where conifers are separated from hardwoods.

Family. Physical features are emphasized in families. This is where dogs are separated from cats in the animal kingdom, and walnuts are differentiated from hickory nuts in plants.

Genus. Organisms are very closely related here. Modern humans, along with the extinct primates *Homo erectus* and *Homo neanderthalensis*, are part of the *Homo* genus.

Species. The final and most specific classification that can interbreed and create offspring. Examples of species include *Homo sapiens*, where the only further differentiations are typically traits such as gender or coloration.

All organisms must be able to grow, reproduce, and maintain stable internal conditions even when the world and environment around them change. Regulation of the organism's internal body allows the organism to survive conditions. Organisms differ in how they regulate their bodies.

The behavior of individual organisms is influenced by internal cues (hunger and internal temperature) and external cues (changes in the environment). Humans and other organisms have senses that help them detect internal and external cues (National Research Council, 2012).

Test Tip

Homeostasis

The tendency to maintain a stable, relatively constant internal environment is called homeostasis. For example, no matter how hot or cold it is outside, the human body will maintain a temp of 98.6 on average, unless there is sickness or infection.

Organism Type	Definition	Types of Animals
Cold-blooded	Animals that have a body temperature varying with that of the environment.	amphibians, reptiles, fish, insects
Warm-blooded	Animals that maintain a constant body temperature, regardless of the temperature in the environment. For example, humans will sweat when they are hot and shiver when they are cold.	Mammals, birds

Circulatory and Respiratory Systems

These systems are responsible for the flow of blood, nutrients, oxygen and other gases, and hormones to and from cells. The circulatory system and respiratory system work together to circulate oxygen and blood throughout the body.

- Heart (cardiovascular)
- Lungs (pulmonary)
- Arteries, veins, coronary and portal vessels (systemic)

Types of Circulatory Systems

Circulatory System	Definition	Animal Types
Open	A primitive circulatory system where blood is pumped into the body cavity and is not enclosed in blood vessels.	Most invertebrates - insects, crustaceans, most mollusks
Closed	A sophisticated system where blood is pumped by the heart and is enclosed in blood vessels.	Most vertebrates – mammals, reptiles, fish, birds

Digestive and Excretory Systems

These systems are responsible taking in food and breaking it up into nutrients the body will use for fuel. It is also responsible for removing the waste left over after the food is processed for nutrients.

- Gastrointestinal tract (stomach and intestines)
- Bladder
- Colon
- Kidneys (filter the blood)

Nervous, Endocrine, and Immune Systems

These systems make up the master control mechanism of the body.

- Brain – hypothalamus, thalamus, and pituitary gland
- Spinal cord
- Neurons
- Hormones

Heredity

Heredity is the passing on of physical or mental characteristics genetically from one generation to another.

A gene is the basic physical and functional unit of heredity. Genes are made up of deoxyribonucleic acid or **DNA**. Genes act as instructions to make molecules called **proteins**. These proteins make cells, which make tissues, which make organs, which make organ systems.

Living things have two copies of each gene, one inherited from each parent. Most genes are the same in all people, but a small number of genes (less than 1 percent of the total) are slightly different among people. These small differences contribute to each person's unique physical features.

Alleles are forms of the same gene with slight differences in their sequence of DNA bases. **Dominance** is when the effect of one phenotype of one allele masks the contribution of a second allele at the same locus. The first allele is dominant, and the second allele is recessive. For example, in humans, brown eye color is dominant over blue eye color. For a person to display blue eyes, she must have both recessive alleles.

Gregor Mendel

Gregor Mendel is known as the Father of Genetics for his work with pea plants in the 1850s and 1860s. Mendel showed that when a true-breeding yellow pea (YY) and a true-breeding green pea (yy) were cross-bred, their offspring always produced yellow seeds. However, in the next generation, the green peas reappeared. To explain this phenomenon, Mendel coined the terms recessive and dominant in reference to certain traits.

Generation 1		
	y	y
Y	Yy	Yy
Y	Yy	Yy

100% of the offspring will be yellow (Y) because yellow is dominant over green (y).

Yy

Generation 2		
	Y	y
Y	YY	Yy
y	Yy	yy

25% of the offspring will be green because the offspring must inherit both recessive alleles to show a green color.

yy

Interdependence of organisms

The continuation of life depends on how organisms interact with each other and their environment. Life can be organized into several different levels of function and complexity. These functional levels are species, populations, communities, and ecosystems (Pidwirny, 2006).

Level	Description	Examples
Species	A group of interbreeding organisms that do not ordinarily breed with members of other groups.	The polar bear (Ursus maritimus) is a hypercarnivorous bear whose native range lies largely within the Arctic Circle.
Populations	Comprises all the individuals of a given species in a specific area or region at a certain time. Populations can evolve over time because of genetic variation.	All the polar bears in the Arctic Circle is the population. Within the population, polar bears contain genetic variance within the species.
Communities	All the populations in a specific area or region at a certain time. There are many interactions among species in a community (food webs).	The polar bears, the penguins, the fish, and the plants make up the community. These all interact when it comes to food and survival.
Ecosystems	The dynamic entities composed of the biological (living) community and the abiotic (nonliving) environment.	The Arctic ecosystem is made up of the water/ice, the animals, and the atmosphere in that area.

Energy pyramids and food webs

Within ecosystems there is an interdependence among organisms of the same or different species. There is also interdependence between living and nonliving elements in the environment. For example, organisms in an ecosystem interact with one another in complex feeding hierarchies, which together represent a food web.

Energy pyramids (or trophic pyramids) show the transfer of energy from one stage of a food chain to another. A **food chain** is a hierarchical structure of organisms that are dependent on each other for food. A **food web** is when multiple food chains are interacting simultaneously.

Producers (plants) produce their own food from sunlight, carbon dioxide, and water. These are usually the bottom tier of the food web or energy pyramid.

Consumers eat their food and are categorized into four main groups:

1. **Primary** consumers are herbivores; they eat plants. In the energy pyramid, the bunny is the primary consumer.

2. **Secondary** consumers eat the primary consumer. In the energy pyramid, the snake is the secondary consumer.

3. **Tertiary** consumers eat the secondary consumers and are usually carnivores (meat-eaters). In the energy pyramid, the bird is the tertiary consumer.

4. **Quaternary** consumers eat the tertiary consumers and are carnivores. In the energy pyramid, the quaternary consumer is the hawk. This food chain ends with the hawk, which would be considered the top carnivore.

Decomposers are organisms that turn dead material, such as an animal carcass or a dead tree, into soil by recycling nutrients as food. Decomposers include earthworms, small soil beetles, fungi, and bacteria.

Carrying capacity is the maximum population of a particular organism that a given environment can support without detrimental effects. Individual survival and population sizes depend on such factors as predation, disease, availability of resources, and parameters of the physical environment. Earth's varied combinations of these factors provide the physical environments in which its ecosystems (e.g., deserts, grasslands, rain forests, and coral reefs) develop and in which the diverse species of the planet live (National Research Council, 2012).

Here is an example of one type of energy pyramid. Keep in mind that there is an energy pyramid for all ecosystems.

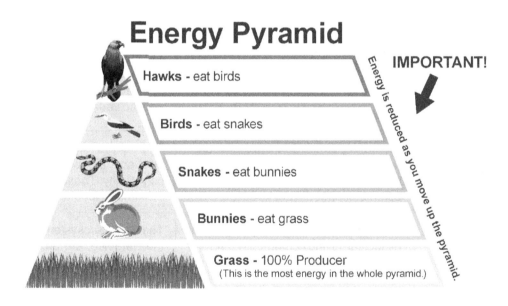

Interaction of organisms

Interactions among organisms may be predatory, competitive, or mutually beneficial. These are referred to as ecological relationships (National Geographic, n.d.).

Relationship	Definition	Example
Competition	When two or more organisms rely on the same environmental resource	Because they eat the same type of food, cheetahs and lions compete within their ecosystem.
Predation	Behavior of one animal feeding on another	The lion eats the zebra. The lion is the predator; the zebra is the prey.
Symbiosis	The close relationship of two dissimilar organisms	There are three type of symbiosis: mutualism, commensalism, and parasitism.
Mutualism	A symbiotic relationship where both organisms benefit	Humans have a mutualistic relationship with micro-organisms. Bacteria in the digestive tract keeps humans healthy while the bacteria are fed by what the human eats.
Commensalism	A symbiotic relationship where one organism benefits and one does not benefit but is unharmed	The cattle egret sits on top of the cattle and eats the bugs that land on the cattle.
Parasitism	A symbiotic relationship where one organism benefits and one is harmed	A tick living on a dog benefits while the dog is harmed.

When put together, all of the above processes comprise an ecosystem, which is a biological community of organisms interacting with their environment and each other.

Pollution

Pollution can impact an environment in a number of ways. It can directly kill organisms, such as an oil spill that prevents water from being reoxygenated and starving waterborne organisms of air. Pollution can also interrupt any of the above interactions, negatively impacting life throughout the ecosystem in a ripple effect.

This page intentionally left blank.

E – Engineering, Technology and Applications of Science

1. Problem solving through inventing solutions to simple problems

1. Problem solving through inventing solutions to simple problems

It is important to show students how they can implement solution to problems. This can be done in a variety of ways, but most importantly, students should understand that trial and error, trying again, thinking about different possibilities, and working with peers are all ways to solve problems. Science is all about inquiry and experimentation to make the world a better place. The following are methods and resources teachers can use to help students solve simple problems in the science classroom.

Manipulatives

Manipulatives are physical objects used as tools to engage students in learning. Examples of manipulatives in elementary science class include things like rocks, magnifying glasses, gears, magnets, scales, and microscopes. Science lessons provide opportunities to use manipulatives in the classroom to engage students in learning activities.

Models

Science teachers can use models to communicate ideas and to represent abstract phenomena. For example, the solar system is impossible to see in a classroom or lab; however, a model of the solar system is easily accessible in a classroom or lab.

Scientific Equipment

Scientific equipment should be maintained in working order to ensure safety and reliability of experiments. Equipment in elementary science class include tools like balances, scales, and stop watches.

Real-Word Examples

Effective teachers find ways to connect their students to the lesson through authentic experiences. Elementary science provides a lot of opportunities to demonstrate real-world examples of scientific phenomena.

Print And Digital Representations

It is important to provide relevant and current information in print and digital formats. This includes maintaining awareness of emerging trends in science education and present these trends in class. Remember backwards design when planning lessons using print and digital content. Make sure your learning objectives are aligned to the standards and the school's goals, and then develop the tasks for the activity.

It is also important to ensure students know how to interpret scientific data from graphs and charts. The table below provides and overview of some graphical representations often used in science materials.

Types of Graphs Used in Science

Graph	How It Is Used	Example
Line	Line charts, or line graphs, are powerful visual tools that illustrate trends in data over a period of time or a particular correlation. This line graph shows population growth in certain species over time. There are three different lines representing three different species.	**POPULATION GROWTH** Species A · Species B · Species C (line graph with values 0 to 1.200.000; x-axis: 1900-1920, 1920-1940, 1940-1960, 1960-1980, 1980-1999)
Bar	One can easily compare two or more variables when using a bar graph. Each bar represents a variable. When the bars are stacked next to each other, it is easy to compare data. This bar graph is comparing carrying capacity of several species in different ecosystems.	**CARRYING CAPACITY BY SPECIES** (bar graph with values 0 to 3.500.000; categories: ALLIGATORS, BIRDS, SNAKES, MAMMALS; legend: Eco A, Eco B, Eco C)
Pie	Pie charts are generally used to show percentage or proportional data. The percentage represented by each category is provided next to the corresponding slice of pie. In this example, the percentages of substances in the atmosphere are broken down.	(pie chart; legend: Nitrogen, Oxygen, Carbon dioxide, Argon)

Technology

Technology can enhance the learning environment in science class. Guidelines for using technology differ from district to district and state to state. It is important for teachers to review their own district's and school's guidelines regarding technology in the classroom.

Virtual Labs

Virtual labs are an effective way to engage students. Students can input data, gather information, and conduct an experiment in a virtual lab. Virtual labs are also helpful because they allow students the experience even if funds are not available for the physical lab.

Technology Tools

Students use a database to find other studies that relate to their topics. Students use a spreadsheet to store their data from an experiment. Students use presentation software like PowerPoint or Keynote to present their findings to the class. Teachers must know when and how to use these tools effectively.

Hands-on Tools

It is important not to over-complicate your approach in this area. Regardless of your school's budget or access to advanced technology, remember that one of your primary goals is teaching stuednts to use tools to understand science. Here are some ideas of how you can use simple resources nearly every classroom has on hand:

- Track weather trends by using a calendar to record temperature, humidity, and precipitation.

- Build interactive tools like kites, pinwheels, or parachutes, then observe and record how different shapes, sizes, and patterns are affected differently by the air.

- Use pictures to track how sunny it is each day, then record daily high and low temperatures and graph them over a set period.

Collaborative strategies

Collaborative strategies, where a lesson is presented by the teacher and then put into practice by the student, maximizes effective instruction. This also gives the teacher the opportunity to identify and correct misconceptions as they see students apply the lessons in a real-life context.

Examples of collaborative activities include the following:

- Using simple experiments where students apply the scientific method themselves. For example, have students work in groups where they plant seeds in three cups, water them at different levels, and then record their observations each day.

- Continually ask students "why." Teach them to refer back to the foundations of their knowledge and tie critical thinking in with each lesson.

- Seek out local scientific or research institutions who would be willing to partner with you in facilitating classroom activities.

Test Tip

Collaborative strategies are **student-centered**, meaning that the student is the focus of the instruction rather than the teacher. Look for answer choices that showcase student engagement and address students' unique learning needs, culture, background, interests, and aspirations.

Questioning and critical thinking

Asking students questions at key points in the lesson is important because it keeps students engaged, develops critical thinking, and allows the teacher to check for understanding at various levels. Questions should go beyond simple recall questions (yes/no questions or low-level questions). The benefits of questioning include:

- Measures student understanding of the material

- Engages students

- Promotes active participation

- Provides opportunities to review, summarize, or emphasize important information

- Fosters critical thinking

Here are some other techniques to help increase critical thinking in the classroom:

- **Wait time.** This involves giving the students time to think and formulate an answer, which is especially important when asking high-level questions.

- **Specific feedback.** Provide feedback using specific language regarding what is correct or incorrect about their answers. For example, "You're on the right track when you say that the plant height is the dependent variable. Now tell me what is influencing the plant height."

- **Redirection.** When student answers are not accurate, try redirection by saying things like, "Have you considered…?" or, "What about…?". This technique allows the students to rethink their responses without feeling defensive about offering an incorrect answer.

- **Probing.** If a student offers a partial answer or if you want to increase the level of questioning, ask probing, follow-up questions. Not all students respond to high cognitive level questions immediately. Start with the concrete and move to the abstract. This technique helps the student ease into deeper thinking.

- **Increasing question complexity.** Ask follow-up questions like, "Why does that happen?" or "What does that look like?" This helps students stretch beyond their comfort zone and think critically.

Just like in English class, science class should give all students an opportunity to engage in socially and culturally responsive topics. Students should have the opportunity to learn about women in science and the contributions all cultures have made in science.

Bias

Textbooks can be biased because they are generally written from the perspective of the dominant culture. Therefore, it is important for teachers to draw from an array of material that explains concepts. Teachers should also try to refrain from inserting any bias into science instruction. Remember, textbooks are resources, NOT the curriculum.

Teachers must also find reputable research to use in their classroom. Resources that are helpful for elementary science instructors include:

- National Science Teacher Association

- Association for Science Teacher Education

- National Earth Science Teacher Association

- Any academic journal with peer-reviewed research

Quick Tip

The main thing to consider when choosing material for the science classroom is the standards. Standards outline what skills students should be able to master based on grade level.

For teachers to be effective in the science classroom, they must have a current and relevant understanding of the research governing the profession. There are several ways to do this:

1. Teachers can join reputable science organizations. These organizations often publish research teachers can use to guide their decisions in the classroom.

2. Teachers can attend professional development that focuses on researched-based strategies in science.

3. Teachers can be data-driven in their decision making.

4. Teachers can engage in lifelong learning practices.

English learners and science instruction

Science is a way to engage with English language learners (ELL). Science, in many ways, transcends language because every student has a sense of wonder and inquiry.

To maximize ELL participation and mastery of science concepts:

- Provide ELL students with science materials in their native language.

- Use translators or paraprofessionals to help you explain complex science concepts in students' native language.

Think about it!

Be careful! If you give students a writing assignment in science, you are also assessing writing in English. Therefore, if you want to measure ELL students' understanding of science concepts, a science diagnostic test in the student's native language is the best way to do that. That way, you are assessing science skills and not English language skills.

This page intentionally left blank.

Science Practice Questions

1. Which of the following is most important in the early childhood science classroom?

    A. Curiosity and inquiry

    B. Diligence and perseverance

    C. Skepticism and cynicism

    D. Interest and happiness

2. These types of waves must travel through a medium. They cannot travel in a vacuum.

    A. Light waves

    B. Electromagnetic waves

    C. Sound waves

    D. Heat waves

3. Which of the following has a head, thorax, and abdomen?

    A. Fish

    B. Ant

    C. Snake

    D. Clam

4. Which of the following has an open circulatory system?

    A. Fish

    B. Cow

    C. Human

    D. Grasshopper

5. The diagram below depicts which of the following Earth's spheres?

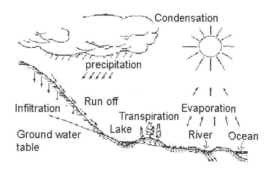

    A. Hydrosphere

    B. Biosphere

    C. Cryosphere

    D. Atmosphere

6. This causes the seasons on Earth.

   A. The Earth's rotation on its axis

   B. The Earth's tilt on its axis

   C. The Earth's revolution around the sun

   D. The Earth's distance from the moon

7. Students are discussing ways to reduce pollution and reduce climate change. Which of the following would be most effective in achieving this?

   A. Reduce the use of water.

   B. Increase the use of products made from recycled items.

   C. Reduce the use of fossil fuels.

   D. Increase the use of electricity.

8. A 1st grade teacher is going over common problems regarding pollution. She asks the students about ways in which they can combat pollution. One student says, "We can drive electric cars." Another says, "We can recycle our plastics." Then another says, "We can reuse things instead of throwing them out." This is an example of which of the following?

   A. Working together as a team to solve a common problem

   B. Brainstorming possible classroom activities for future science labs

   C. Debating what causes certain problems in the world

   D. Recognizing situations where change and improvement can be applied to solve problems

9. Which of the following is an example of a chemical change?

   A. Boiling water

   B. Evaporation

   C. Rust

   D. Melting ice

10. A teacher brings in different types of rocks for students to pass around and make observations. Which of the following would be an example of an observation that would aid in classifying the rocks?

   A. "These rocks are very pretty!"

   B. "I like this rock better than this other rock."

   C. "This rock feels smooth, and this rock feels rough."

   D. "I have rocks like this in my backyard."

Number	Answer	Explanation
1.	A	In the science classroom, students must have a sense of curiosity and inquiry. The word inquiry is synonymous with science because students must observe, ask, questions, form hypotheses, and draw conclusions. Teachers must help students develop a sense of curiosity and inquiry to do this.
2.	C	Sound energy is produced by vibrations and travels only through a medium—solid, liquid or gas.
3.	B	Insects have a head, thorax, and abdomen. The only insect listed in the answer choices is an ant.
4.	D	Invertebrates have open circulatory systems. The only invertebrate listed is a grasshopper. With an open circulatory system, the animal does not need gills or lungs. Oxygen enters the body through holes in the body. Air enters the grasshopper's body through structures called spiracles.
5.	A	The diagram shows the water cycle, which is the hydrosphere.
6.	B	Seasons on Earth are a result of the Earth's tilt on its axis. When the Northern Hemisphere is tilted toward the sun, it is summer. When the Norther Hemisphere is tilted away from the sun, it is winter. The same is true for the Southern hemisphere.
7.	C	The burning of fossil fuels increases levels of which causes climate change.
8.	D	Answer D defines what the students are doing. The problem they recognize is pollution. Then they come up with improvements that can be made to solve the problem. Answer A is incorrect because they are not working together to solve the problem; they are simply talking about things they could do to reduce pollution. Answer B is incorrect because they are not thinking about future classroom labs. Answer C is incorrect because they are not debating.
9.	C	Rust is an example of a chemical change. Boiling water, evaporation, and ice melting are physical changes.
10.	C	Rock texture is one way to classify and organize rocks. None of the other observations would help with classification of rocks.

IV. SCIENCE

V. Health and Physical Education, Creative and Performing Arts

A – Health and Physical Education

1. Health
2. Physical Education

1. Health

The Centers for Disease Control and Prevention (CDC) has outlined performance indicators for the National Health Education Standards (NHES). These performance indicators were developed to establish, promote, and support health-enhancing behaviors for students in all grade levels, from prekindergarten through grade 12. The NHES provides a framework for teachers, administrators, and policymakers in designing or selecting curricula, allocating instructional resources, and assessing student achievement and progress. Importantly, the standards provide students, families, and communities with concrete expectations for health education.

Standard	Indicator	Early Childhood Application
1	Students will comprehend concepts related to health promotion and disease prevention to enhance health.	Describe ways to prevent common childhood injuries and health problems. Describe when it is important to seek healthcare.
2	Students will analyze the influence of family, peers, culture, media, technology, and other factors on health behaviors.	Identify how peers can influence healthy and unhealthy behaviors. Describe how the school and community can support personal health practices and behaviors.
3	Students will demonstrate the ability to access valid information, products, and services to enhance health.	Identify trusted adults and professionals who can help promote health. Identify ways to locate school and community health helpers.
4	Students will demonstrate the ability to use interpersonal communication skills to enhance health and avoid or reduce health risks.	Demonstrate refusal skills that avoid or reduce health risks. Demonstrate nonviolent strategies to manage or resolve conflict.
5	Students will demonstrate the ability to use decision-making skills to enhance health.	Differentiate between situations when a health-related decision can be made individually or when assistance is needed.
6	Students will demonstrate the ability to use goal-setting skills to enhance health.	Set a personal health goal and track progress toward its achievement. Identify resources to assist in achieving a personal health goal.
7	Students will demonstrate the ability to practice health-enhancing behaviors and avoid or reduce health risks.	Demonstrate healthy practices and behaviors to maintain or improve personal health. Demonstrate behaviors that avoid or reduce health risks.
8	Students will demonstrate the ability to advocate for personal, family, and community health.	Express opinions and give accurate information about health issues. Encourage others to make positive health choices.

Basic Structure of the Human Body

There are 11 organ systems in the human body: integumentary system, skeletal system, muscular system, lymphatic system, respiratory system, digestive system, nervous system, endocrine system, cardiovascular system, urinary system, and reproductive systems. For this exam, you will need to know the following:

- **Skeletal System** – These are bones, and they support the body's internal organs. For example, the ribs support and protect the heart and lungs. Students should be aware that a strong skeletal system is important and can be achieved with nutrition and exercise.

- **Muscular System** – This includes the skeletal, smooth and cardiac muscles. This system is responsible for carrying out body movements.

- **Cardiovascular system** – This includes the heart that pumps blood and blood vessels such as arteries and veins, that transport the blood to every part of our body providing organs and muscles with nourishment. The blood carries oxygen, carbon dioxide, nutrients, waste and more throughout the body. It is important to communicate that to avoid disease, students should work on their cardiac health through nutrition and exercise.

- **Nervous System** – This includes the brain, spinal cord, and nerves. Stress can negatively affect the nervous system. Play, physical activity, yoga, and meditation are all beneficial to a healthy nervous system.

Nutrition

The best place to find reputable research for guiding instruction in nutrition is the United States Department of Agriculture MyPlate. MyPlate is a website where people can find nutritional guidelines and information on healthy eating. The organization has presented information easy to understand by using a plate rather than a chart or graph. The idea is that healthy eating includes a plate that look like the one below.

Macromolecules in Food

Macromolecules are the large molecules found in our food. They are the source of nutrients and energy. The three macromolecules found in food are carbohydrates, proteins, and fats.

- **Carbohydrates** – Composed of sugars and are the body's first source of energy. Fuel from carbohydrates is available to the body immediately. If not used, they are stored in the body and can become fat. are

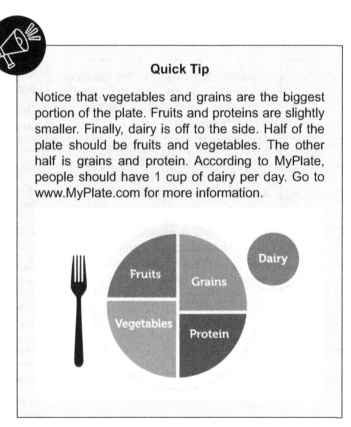

Quick Tip

Notice that vegetables and grains are the biggest portion of the plate. Fruits and proteins are slightly smaller. Finally, dairy is off to the side. Half of the plate should be fruits and vegetables. The other half is grains and protein. According to MyPlate, people should have 1 cup of dairy per day. Go to www.MyPlate.com for more information.

- **Proteins** – Composed of amino acids, proteins help to build cell structures in the body. Eating protein is essential for building muscle.

- **Lipids (fats)** – The main way the body stores energy. In food, there are many types of fats— saturated, unsaturated, polyunsaturated, monounsaturated, and trans fats.

2. Physical Education

When teaching physical education (PE), it is important to understand the 3 domains of learning and how they apply to physical activity.

1. **Cognitive Domain** – The cognitive domain has to do with mental skills and the acquisition of knowledge. An example of how this is used in PE is when students are learning the rules of a game or listening to directions before a physical activity.

2. **Psychomotor Domain** – The psychomotor domain is the physical domain. This includes both gross motor skills (large muscles) and fine motor skills (small muscles). An example of how this is used in PE is when students are engaged in a physical activity like running, jumping, playing, etc.

3. **Affective Domain** – The affective domain has to do with feelings, emotions, self-esteem and how children see themselves. This domain finds its way into all types of learning, but especially sports. Some example of using the affective domain in PE are teaching students not to give up, to use good sportsmanship, to share, to help their teammates, etc.

Test Tip

In the PE and arts section of the exam, be on the lookout for answer choices that nurture the affective domain. Remember, a big part of teaching young students is helping them understand their feelings and the feelings of others, so answer choices that include the affective domain are typically good answer choices.

Components of health-related fitness

It is important to understand the components of health and fitness when teaching young students. There are several areas you will be tested on for this portion of the test: fine motor skills, gross motor skills, and types of fitness.

Fine Motor Skills

Fine motor skills involve the small muscles in the hands and fingers. Activities that use fine motor skills are handwriting, drawing, and painting.

Gross Motor skills

Gross motor skills involve the large muscles in the legs, arms, and torso. Activities that involve gross motor skills are running, dancing, and jumping.

Types of fitness

- **Muscular strength and endurance** - Muscular strength and endurance are two important parts of the body's ability to move, lift things, and conduct day-to-day activities. Muscular strength is the amount of force you can put out or the amount of weight you can lift. Muscular endurance is how many times you can do the activity without getting tired. Activities include weightlifting and pushing or pulling something.

- **Cardiovascular fitness** – Cardiovascular is related to the circulatory system—the heart and blood vessels that carry nutrients and oxygen to the tissues of the body and removes carbon dioxide and other wastes. Activities include running, aerobics, swimming, etc.

- **Flexibility** – Flexibility is the ability of a joint or series of joints to move through an unrestricted, pain-free range of motion. Activities include stretching and yoga.

- **Body composition** – Body composition is a method of breaking down the body into its core components: fat, protein, minerals, and body water. It describes weight accurately in terms of what the body is made up of.

Think about it!

Practices for body composition should be done in private because they involve fat measurements and weight. Conducting this in front of the entire class can be traumatizing to students. Be sure to refrain from whole-group body composition analysis.

For the early childhood exam, it is important to understand the 6 elements of physical fitness and how they are applied in the early childhood classroom.

6 Elements of Physical Fitness

1. **Agility** – the capacity to change course, controlling the direction and position of your body while maintaining your momentum. For example, running straight and then pivoting and running in the other direction involves agility.

2. **Balance** – the ability to stabilize your body. For example, standing on one foot or walking across a beam requires balance.

3. **Coordination** – the synchronization of your senses and your body parts in a way that enhances motor skills. For example, playing ping pong or dribbling a basketball require coordination.

4. **Speed** – the ability to move swiftly and efficiently. For example, running in a race requires speed.

5. **Power** – the combination of speed and force. Throwing heavy objects or lifting something heavy requires power.

6. **Reaction time** – how swiftly you interpret and then react to expected and unexpected events happening around you. Hearing the starter pistol and exploding of the starting line requires reaction time.

Quick Tip

Remember, physical activity is essential in student learning. Students need brain breaks where they get up and move their bodies. Physical activity not only helps students stay healthy, but it also helps students make sense of the world. Teamwork, communication, execution, and perseverance are all skills taught in a PE class. Physical activity should be as important as everything else in the early childhood classroom.

B – Creative and Performing Arts

1. Purposes and Functions of the Arts
2. Structure and Processes Within the Arts

1. Purposes and Functions of the Arts

Artistic activities in the early childhood classroom help children understand all subjects such as reading and math by promoting visual, motor, and social development. Teachers should use art as a mechanism for expression and as a communication tool. Different types of art can reveal children's thoughts, feelings, and interests. Engaging in artistic activities allows children to externalize their feelings.

Music

Listening to and making music help children develop their intellectual, auditory, sensory, speech, and motor skills.

Drawing and Painting

Drawing and painting are beneficial for young students because these activities help develop fine motor skills. Drawing and painting also help to reinforce skills in writing, reading, and creativity. Drawing and painting also help to boost self-esteem because students are able to express themselves.

Quick Tip

Research shows that engaging in the arts—drawing, painting, sculpting, acting, singing, playing—enhances students' abilities in all disciplines like math, science, social studies, and English language arts.

Theater

Activities in theater encourages children to see themselves in the characters of books. Students learn to identify with characters by living their experiences. Theater helps students comprehend complex stories and helps students empathize with characters. Theater is play, and play is essential in the early childhood classroom.

2. Structure and Processes Within the Arts

For the exam, you will be required to know the basic terminology, elements, principles, materials, and processes used in visual art, music, dance, and theater.

Drawing and Painting

A big part of teaching art is introducing students to color. You will most likely encounter questions about the color wheel on the exam. The color wheel was developed by Sir Isaac Newton, and it is a color spectrum using a circle. If you follow the wheel from the top and then clockwise, the colors are red, orange, yellow, green, blue, indigo, and violet.

The color wheel is made up of three different types of colors - Primary, Secondary, and Tertiary.

- **Primary** - There are 3 primary colors – red, blue, yellow. They are called primary because no two colors can be mixed to make red, blue, or yellow. All colors on the color wheel are the result of mixing the primary colors.

- **Secondary** – There are 3 secondary colors – orange, green, purple. They are called secondary because they are a result of mixing the primary colors. For example, orange is a mix of red and yellow. Green is a mix of blue and yellow. Finally, purple is a mix of red and blue.

- **Tertiary** – There are 6 tertiary colors – red-purple, red-orange, blue-green, yellow-green, blue-purple, and yellow-orange. The proper way to list tertiary colors is primary color-secondary color.

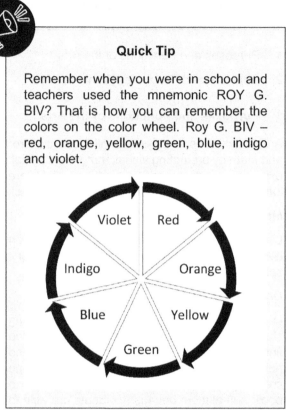

Quick Tip

Remember when you were in school and teachers used the mnemonic ROY G. BIV? That is how you can remember the colors on the color wheel. Roy G. BIV – red, orange, yellow, green, blue, indigo and violet.

Arts Creation

Line, shape, and texture are also important elements in art. Students use these elements to express themselves in drawing and painting. Line engages the eye and can be short, long, thin, thick, etc. Teachers can also emphasize shape when teaching art. For example, emphasizing geometric shapes incorporates math into art class. Finally, texture can be beneficial in class because it encourages students to use different substances. This aligns to science because rocks have different textures.

Music

Music engages all areas of child development and skills for school readiness, including intellectual, social-emotional, motor, language, and literacy. Exposing children to music during early development helps them learn the sounds and meanings of words. Rhyming music can help students with phonemic awareness. Songs can help students remember complex concepts. Finally, music can accompany stories so students can comprehend meaning.

On the exam, you might encounter questions about the basic concepts of music.

- **Harmony** – the combination of simultaneously sounded musical notes to produce chords and chord progressions that have a pleasing effect. For example, when one person sings low and the other high at the same time and the result is pleasing to the ear.

- **Melody** – a series of notes played in an order that is memorable and recognizable as a separate unit. For example, the melody of *Row, Row Row Your Boat* is easily recognizable to most people.

- **Rhythm** – a strong, regular, repeated pattern of movement or sound. Rhythm can be used to reinforce poetry and is helpful in remembering songs.

- **Tempo** – the speed at which the music is played. For example, a tempo of 60 beats per minute signifies one beat per second, while a tempo of 120 beats per minute is twice as rapid.

- **Pitch** – the position of a single sound in the complete range of sound. Pitch is measured by frequency. For example, a high frequency is perceived as a high pitch and a low frequency as a low pitch.

Other Principles of Art Creation

- **Contrast** – refers to the arrangement of opposite elements and effects. For example, light and dark colors, smooth and rough textures, large and small shapes. Contrast can be used to create variety, visual interest, and drama in an artwork.

- **Balance** – refers to the use of artistic elements such as line, texture, color, and form in the creation of art in a way that is visually stable. For example, when students draw certain shapes, they will use balance, so the shapes are pleasing to the eye.

- **Unity** – refers to how different elements of design work together and create a sense of unity. This can be achieved through proximity, simplicity, repetition and continuation.

- **Scale** – refers to the size of an object in relationship to another object. In art, early childhood students tend to compare the size of objects to the size of their own bodies as a reference.

- **Movement** – refers to the path the viewer's eye takes through the work of art, tending to move towards focal areas. Movement can be directed along lines, edges, shape, and color.

- **Pattern** – refers to a design in which lines, shapes, forms or colors are repeated. The part that is repeated is called a motif. Patterns can be regular or irregular. This is helpful when integrating art and math skills in early childhood classrooms.

This page intentionally left blank.

1. Which of the following activities would support dramatic play in a classroom of 3-year-olds?

   A. Read a play to students and analyze each character.

   B. Allow students to dress up as their favorite character and act out a scene in the play.

   C. Have students read a play in cooperative groups.

   D. Have students listen to a play in their listening center.

2. Which of the following activities would help 1st grade students see how geometric shapes are used in art?

   A. Have students read about geometric shapes and art in their textbooks.

   B. Have an expert in abstract art come in and speak to the class.

   C. Provide students a set of cardboard geometric shapes and have them make a piece of art.

   D. Watch a movie about famous artists who use geometric shapes in their art.

3. Students are working in groups to draw scenes from different cultures. The scenes depict food, celebrations, and family. Which of the following does this activity support?

   A. Students will recognize that even though the food or celebrations may be different, cultures are alike in how we eat, celebrate and love.

   B. Students will emphasize the differences among cultures and how those differences lead to conflict.

   C. Students will learn proper artistic expression by using cultural activities.

   D. Students will see how families are different in different places around the world.

4. Which of the following activities would increase students gross motor skills?

   A. Hopping

   B. Writing

   C. Sewing

   D. Drawing

5. A teacher of 2-year-old students is using poems that rhyme to help students identify similar sounds. They all recite the poems and emphasize the parts that rhyme. The teacher is helping students work on what skill?

   A. Phonics

   B. Phonological awareness

   C. Vocabulary

   D. Phonemic Awareness

6. Which of the following helps to increase prekindergarten students' curiosity and inquiry skills?

    A. Reading

    B. Writing

    C. Playing

    D. Singing

7. A 1st grade teacher is having trouble getting students to sit quietly for story time. This usually happens after lunch. Which of the following is the best way to rectify this situation?

    A. Reprimand students and put their name on the board when they misbehave.

    B. Use short breaks to allow the students to move and expend energy.

    C. Call home to the parents and ask for help at home.

    D. Use a system of rewards to get students to comply to the rules.

8. Mr. Rodriguez is a prekindergarten PE teacher. He is having a hard time getting students to understand different rules of soccer. He has told them over and over, but they still do not seem to understand. What can Mr. Rodriguez do to fix this situation?

    A. Model different scenarios of the game.

    B. Give students a handout to accompany the rules presentation.

    C. Ask the assistant principal to help.

    D. Start the game with no rules because the students are not ready yet.

9. Which of the following would be the most effective activity for self-expression in a classroom of 2-year-olds? Choose all that apply.

    A. Reading

    B. Writing

    C. Dancing

    D. Drawing

10. Ms. Jensen is helping her students understand energy during a lesson in PE. She tells them that the foods they eat are directly related to the energy they have. Which of the following is the main source of energy used by the body in the first few minutes of exercise?

    A. Protein

    B. Carbohydrates

    C. Fats

    D. Amino acids

Number	Answer	Explanation
1.	B	Answer B is the only choice where students are acting out the play and is, therefore, the correct answer. Remember, activities that support exploration and play are good answer choices on the exam.
2.	C	Application is always going to be the best answer on these exams. In this case, students are engaging in art, which is much more effective than reading about it or listening to someone talk about it. Precutting shapes for the students ensures they are using geometric shapes.
3.	A	Answer A is the best answer for several reasons. First, it emphasizes that we are more alike than different, a common theme on this exam. Second, the students are celebrating other cultures in this activity.
4.	A	Gross motor skills use the large muscles in the torso, arms, and legs to complete whole-body movements. Therefore, answer choice A is the correct answer. Answer choices B, C, and D are all fine motor skills activities.
5.	D	Rhyme directly relates to the sounds in words. Therefore, phonemic awareness is the best answer. Quick tip: usually rhyme is associated with phonemic awareness on teacher certification exams.
6.	C	Playing is the best way to cultivate inquiry, curiosity, and imagination.
7.	B	Little kids need breaks to move their bodies so they can concentrate. Therefore, answer B is the best answer. Answers A and C are punitive and never the correct answer. Answer D uses extrinsic rewards, which is on the bad words list.
8.	A	Modeling short scenarios is the most effective approach for this situation. This way, students can see how the rules playout in application. A handout will do little to fix the problem because these are prekindergartners. Asking the assistant principal for help is usually never the correct answer. Finally, forgoing the rules is lowering the standards. Students still need to learn the rules, they just need a different way to understand them.
9.	C, D	Both answers C and D provide students an opportunity to express themselves. You may be tempted to choose writing, but you must keep in mind the age of the students. Writing is not typically a form of expression in 2-year-olds.
10.	B	Carbohydrates are the body's main sources of energy. Carbohydrates are broken down into smaller sugars (glucose, fructose, and galactose) to be used as energy for immediate tasks.

Quick Reference
Guides

Good Words List

Our methodology at is to identify what we call *good words* in the answer choices to determine correct and incorrect answers. Good words are terms and phrases taken from the test specifications that highlight best practices. If you see these words or phrases related to these words in answer choices on the exam, slow down and have a closer look. There is a good possibility these words are in the correct answer choice. We have also included a list of bad words and phrases to avoid. These are typically not the correct answer choice on the exam.

Good Words and Phrases

Accommodations. Modifying instruction or using supports to help special education students achieve. Accommodations do NOT involve lowering the standard or delaying learning.

Action research. The process of evaluating data in the classroom to identify issues and implementing effective and quick actions to solve problems.

Allocating resources. Portioning resources so all students have equal opportunity and time while balancing curriculum and instruction.

Assessments. Using formative and summative data to monitor progress and measure outcomes.

Authentic instruction. Providing students with meaningful, relevant, and useful learning experiences and activities.

Balanced literacy. Reading and writing instruction that uses a variety of literary genres including literary and informational texts.

Bilingual instruction. Helping students use elements of their first language to support learning in English.

Celebrate culture. Finding materials and resources to celebrate the different cultures represented in your classroom.

Classroom management. A variety of skills and techniques that teachers use to keep students organized, orderly, focused, attentive, on task, and academically productive during class.

Collaborative learning. These are strategies that are student-centered and self-directed rather than led by the teacher. Collaboration can also be working with colleagues or stakeholders to improve, create, or produce something.

Comprehensible education. Making information and lessons understandable to students by accommodating and using ancillary materials to help with language barriers.

Concept map. Visual representation of content. Especially useful for illustrating concepts like cause and effect, problem and solution, compare and contrast, etc.

Consent Decree. Protects students' right to a free, comprehensible education. It addresses civil and academic rights of English language learners (ELLs) and requires instruction be delivered in a comprehensible manner so all students can fully participate.

Critical thinking. Higher-order thinking skills that involve evaluating, analyzing, creating, and applying knowledge.

Cultural responsiveness. Instruction as a pedagogy that empowers students intellectually, socially, and emotionally by celebrating and learning about other cultures. This includes recognizing the importance of including students' cultural references in all aspects of learning and designing a productive learning environment.

Data driven decisions. Using scores, writing samples, observations, and other types of qualitative and quantitative data to make instructional decisions.

Depth of knowledge. Framework that is used to identify the cognitive complexity of a problem.

Developmentally appropriate instruction (DAP). Choosing text, tools, and activities that are appropriate for the students' grade level.

Differentiated instruction. Providing all learners in a diverse classroom with different methods to understand instruction.

Diversity as an asset. Seeing diversity in the classroom as an opportunity to learn new things through the perspectives of others.

Evidenced-based. Providing instruction using materials with the best scientific evidence available.

Follow the IEP. A student's individualized education program (IEP) is a legal document. If you see IEP in the answer choices, it is most likely the correct answer.

High expectations for ALL learners. Holding all students to high academic standards regardless of the students' achievement level, ethnicity, language, socioeconomic status.

Horizontal alignment. Organization and coordination of standards and learning goals across content areas in the same grade level.

Inclusive. Providing students with resources and experiences that represent their culture and ethnicity.

Informal learning. Supporting students with self-directed, collaborative learning outside of the classroom.

Interdisciplinary activities. Activities that connect two or more content areas; promotes relevance and critical thinking.

Intrinsic motivation. Answers that promote autonomy, relatedness, and competence are ways to apply intrinsic motivation. Be on the lookout for these answer choices.

Metacognition. Analysis of your own thinking.

Modeling. Demonstrating the application of a skill or knowledge.

Modifications. Changes to the curriculum and learning environment in accordance to a student's IEP. Modifications change the expectations for learning and the level of assessment.

Outcomes. The results of a program, strategy, or resources implemented in the classroom.

Performance assessment. An activity assigned to students to assess their mastery of multiple learning goals aligned to standards.

Play. In early childhood and beyond, play is essential in learning and understanding.

Primary resource. These are materials and information in their original form like diaries, journals, songs, paintings, and autobiographies.

Prior knowledge. What students know about a topic from their previous experiences and learning.

Progress monitor. Keeping track of student or whole class learning in real time. Quantifiable measures of progress, conferring, observing, exit tickets, and student self-assessments.

Relevance, real-world, and relatable. Be sure to choose answers that promote real-world application and make learning relatable to students' lives.

Reliable. Consistent. Producing consistent results under similar conditions.

Remediation. Correcting or changing something to make it better.

Rigorous. A word used to describe curriculum that is challenging and requires students to use higher-order thinking skills.

Scaffolding. Using supports to help students achieve a standard that they would not achieve on their own.

Secondary resource. These are materials and information derived from the original like newspaper articles, history textbooks, and reviews.

Specific and meaningful feedback. More than just a grade at the top of a paper, effective feedback includes positive aspects and how students can apply those positive aspects to improving. In addition, feedback should contain specific things the student should do to improve.

Standards-aligned. Ensuring that curriculum and instruction is aligned to the state-adopted standards.

Student centered/learner centered. A variety of educational programs, learning experiences, instructional approaches, and academic-support strategies that address students' distinct learning needs, interests, or cultural backgrounds.

Validity. Accuracy. How accurately knowledge or skills are measured.

Vertical alignment. Organization of standards and learning goals across grade levels. Structure for which learning and understanding is built from grade level to grade level.

Vocabulary in-context. Always teach vocabulary in context. It helps to relate the vocabulary to the real-world.

Wait time. Time between a question and when a student is called on or a response to a student's reply.

Bad Words and Phrases

Bias. Inserting personal beliefs, stereotypes, and assumptions in the learning process. This can also include learning materials developed from the perspective of the dominant culture that exclude minority perspectives.

Call the parents, principal, district, etc. You are expected to effectively manage your classroom without deferring responsibilities to others. In real life, teachers will often need to call the parents or principal. But on this exam, avoid answer choices that defer responsibilities to someone other than the teacher.

Extra homework. On this exam, students should be getting all of the instruction they need in class. In real life, we all assign homework. However, on this exam, extra homework is not the correct answer choice.

Extrinsic motivators. These are rewards of extrinsic value like pizza parties, recess time, etc. Students should be motivated by intrinsic motivators like self-confidence, sense of accomplishment, and feeling successful.

Hiring a contractor or external vendor. Anytime the answer choice includes using an outside resource like a contractor or a vendor to provide instruction or classroom management, this is typically not the correct answer choice. You are expected to be able to manage your own classroom using your own skills and capabilities.

Homework. Assigning homework is not a preferred strategy on this exam, especially when students are struggling with the material.

Homogenous grouping. Grouping by gender, English proficiency, or learning level is never a best practice on this exam or in your classroom. Homogenous groups should only be used in special circumstances and on a temporary basis.

Punitive solutions. Avoid answer choices that sound like punishments. For this exam, teachers are expected to be implementing positive behavior support methods so avoid any answer choices that sounds punitive.

Silent Independent Reading. Usually, this practice is attached to struggling readers. This would not be an effective practice because if they are struggling, reading independently is not going to help the student get better.

Student aides. Using students as translators or support for special education or ELL students is never a best practice in the classroom.

This page intentionally left blank.

Assessments

The first important thing you can do in preparing for this exam is to understand the different types of assessments. The following table outlines assessment types and how they are used to drive instructional decisions.

Types of Assessments

Assessment Type	Definition	Example
Diagnostic	A pre-assessment providing instructors with information about students' prior knowledge, preconceptions, and misconceptions before beginning a learning activity.	Before starting a reading unit on earth space science, a teacher gives a quick assessment to determine students' prior knowledge of concepts in the text. She uses this information to make instructional decisions moving forward.
Formative	A range of formal and informal assessments or checks conducted by the teacher before, during, and after the learning process in order to modify instruction.	A teacher walks around the room checking on students as they read. She might also write anecdotal notes to review later to help her design further instruction.
Summative	An assessment that focuses on the outcomes. It is frequently used to measure the effectiveness of a program, lesson, or strategy.	A reading teacher gives a midterm exam at the end of the semester.
Performance-based	An assessment that measures students' ability to apply the skills and knowledge learned from a unit or units of study; the task challenges students to use their higher-order, critical thinking skills to create a product or complete a process.	After reading text about the Civil War, students develop stories about different historical figures in the war. Students then perform these stories in front of the class and answer questions.
Criterion-referenced	An assessment that measures student performance against a fixed set of predetermined criteria or learning standards.	At the end of the spring semester, students take the Florida Standards Assessment. The state uses the scores for accountability measures.
Norm-referenced (percentile)	An assessment or evaluation that yields an estimate of the position of the tested individual in a predefined population with respect to the trait being measured.	The NAEP is an exam given every few years for data purposes only to compare students' reading scores across the U.S.
Screening	An assessment used to place students in appropriate classrooms or grade level.	Students are typically screened throughout the year to determine at what level they are reading. Placement decisions are made based on the outcomes of the screening.

ASSESSMENTS

Authentic assessments

There are also other assessments called authentic assessments. These are different from multiple-choice tests in that students have to apply their learning. These assessments come in all forms. The following are a few you will see referenced on the exam. These will be referred to as authentic assessments and alternative assessments.

Oral assessments. Assessments that are conducted, either wholly or in part, by word of mouth. Oral assessments include:

- Answering questions orally
- Performances
- Presentations
- Role-play

Written assessments. Assessments where students write to communicate their learning. Written assessments often yield more information than a multiple-choice test. Teachers should use rubrics to assess written assessments. Written assessments include:

- Essays
- Lab write-up
- Letters
- Journals

Reading Practices

On the exam, you may see questions that reference specific activities in the classroom. We have found that many people new to teaching do not know these activities. This can cause confusion on test day. Therefore, we have provided a list of practices often used in the classroom, especially the early childhood literacy classroom. This is by no means a complete list; there are an infinite number of practices teachers can use. However, this is a list of common practices you may see on the exam.

Reading Fluency Activities

Fluency Strategy	Definition	Example
Basal reading	Leveled reading books	Dick and Jane series
Running records	Assessing students' fluency by determining the student's rate or how many words per min (wpm) a student reads correctly.	Following along as a student reads and marking when he or she makes a mistake or miscues. At the end, the teacher counts how many words per min (wpm) the student read correctly.
Miscue analysis	Looking over the running record, analyzing why the student miscued and employing strategies to help the student with miscues.	After a fluency read, the teacher and student analyze the mistakes the student made and come up with strategies to fix those mistakes.
Repeated reading	Reading text over and over again to help with fluency.	The teacher has a student read a passage and then re-read the passage several times over the course of a week to build automaticity and reading confidence.
Readers theater	A strategy for developing reading fluency. It engages students by having students read parts of a script.	Students are reading a story; each student is one of the characters in the book. Students read aloud through the text.
Choral reading	Reading aloud in unison through a piece of text.	The teacher uses choral reading with ELL students to help them with fluency and confidence.
Silent sustained reading (Usually NOT the correct answer)	Students read silently on their own.	The teacher dedicates 15 minutes every day to having students read their novels on their own.
Popcorn reading (Usually NOT the correct answer)	Spontaneously calling on students to read aloud.	The teacher reads. The teacher spontaneously calls out a student's name, and that student reads aloud until the teacher calls on another student.

Reading Comprehensions Activities

The following table outlines comprehension and higher-order thinking activities that help to increase students' reading comprehension. You will see these activities on the exam in scenario questions.

Activity	Definition	Example
Jigsaw	A cooperative learning activity in which each student or group of students reads and analyzes a small piece of information that is part of a much larger piece. The students then share what they learned with the class.	Teachers arrange students in groups. Each group reads and analyzes a piece of a text. Group members then join with members of other groups, and each student shares and discusses his or her section of the text. As the group shares, the entire text is covered. It is referred to as Jigsaw because students complete the puzzle when they share their individual pieces.
Read aloud/ think aloud.	Teacher or student reads and stops to think aloud about what the text means.	A teacher is reading aloud through difficult text. She gets to a concept that is complex. She stops and models her thought process aloud to show students how to think about their thinking process.
SQ3R	Survey, Question, Read, Recite, Review	Before reading, students look over headings, charts and graphs. Then students turn the headings into questions. Then students read, reread, and review and answer the questions.
Question answer relationship (QAR)	QAR is an approach to reading comprehension where students generate reading questions.	While reading, students consider different types of questions, such as think and search questions, main idea questions, and text-to-self questions.
Chunking	A reading activity that involves breaking down a difficult text into manageable pieces.	In a science class, students break down a lengthy and complex chapter on genetics by focusing on pieces of the text. The teacher has planned for students to read and analyze the text one paragraph at a time.
Think-pair-share	A cooperative learning activity in which students work together to solve a problem or answer a question.	Think – The teacher asks a specific question about the text. Students "think" about what they know or have learned about the topic. Pair – Students pair up to read and discuss. Share - Students share what they've learned in their pairs. Teachers can then expand the "share" into a whole-class discussion.
Reading response journal	A writing activity where students use journals to react to what they read by expressing how they feel and asking questions about the text.	After reading a chapter of a book in class, the teacher asks students to use their reading response journals to respond to the story emotionally, make associations between ideas in the text and their own ideas, and record questions they may have about the story.

Activity	Definition	Example
Double entry journal	A journal activity where students divide their paper in two parts: questions and answers.	Students are reading about China and its culture. Students split their paper in half longways. On one side they generate questions before they read. On the other side, they answer questions as they read.
Dialogue journal	A chance for students to communicate with their teacher or others in writing.	A student is shy in class and doesn't like to raise his hand. The teacher uses a dialogue journal with the student. The student writes the teacher notes about the lesson, and the teacher responds in the journal.
Evidence-based discussion	The teacher sets the expectation that students use evidence in the text to support claims they make during the discussion.	The class is discussing World War II. Students are asking and answering questions. When making claims, students identify support for those claims in the text.
Literature circles	A small-group, cooperative learning activity where students engage and discuss a piece of literature/text.	In their cooperative groups, students read and analyze text together. Each student contributes to the learning. There is an administrator who decides when to read and when to stop and discuss. There is a note taker who writes down important information. There are 2 readers who take turns reading the text based on the administrator's suggestions.
Cloze reading	A passage with certain items, words, or signs removed (cloze text), where the student is asked to replace the missing word with the correct word.	Cloze reading requires the student to understand context and vocabulary in order to identify the correct language or part of speech that belongs in the deleted portions of the text. In addition, the student has to have comprehension of the text in order to write the correct word or words to go in the deleted portions of the text.
Graphic organizers	A pedagogical tool that uses visual symbols to express knowledge and concepts through relationships between them.	Students are filling out a Venn diagram to organize similarities and differences between two characters in the text.

Practice Test

1. When a student has awareness of phonemes in words, syllables, onset-rime segments, and spelling, he or she is demonstrating:

   A. Phonological awareness

   B. Phonics mastery

   C. Phonemic awareness

   D. Structural analysis

2. Phonemic awareness includes the ability to:

   A. Form compound words and combine word parts

   B. Spell accurately and decode unfamiliar words

   C. Pronounce individual sounds in words

   D. Differentiate between homonyms and spell accurately

3. Which of the following set of words is most appropriate if the teacher is focusing on morphology during reading instruction?

   A. Pizza, system, tragedy

   B. Track, trade, trophy

   C. Cat, bat, sat

   D. Unbelievable, irreplaceable, disrespectful

4. Which is NOT a best practice for vocabulary instruction?

   A. Model using context clues

   B. Teaching prefixes, suffixes, and roots

   C. Explicit instruction using a dictionary

   D. Using word walls for target vocabulary

5. A teacher is helping students use the semantic cueing system. Which of the following questions aligns with the semantic cueing system?

   A. Is that structured properly?

   B. What sound does that letter make?

   C. Does that make sense?

   D. Is that a long /a/ sound or short /a/ sound?

6. Students see the following image and say, "Bug!" What stage of word recognition are the students in?

   A. Pre-alphabetic

   B. Partial alphabetic

   C. Full-alphabetic

   D. Consolidated alphabetic

7. If a teacher wants students to understand etymology, which group of words would be most appropriate to analyze?

   A. Cat, bat, sat, trap

   B. Uneven, unruly, undone

   C. Station, transition, lamination

   D. Prescription, transcript, manuscript

8. When students read a text together and then analyze the meaning, what kind of strategy are they using?

   A. Shared reading

   B. Choral reading

   C. Repeated reading

   D. Round robin reading

9. When students memorize high-frequency words, they are engaging in:

   A. Decoding

   B. Onset rime

   C. Sight word recognition

   D. Structural analysis

10. Metacognition is an important skill students need to comprehend text. What activity would be best to foster metacognition in students?

   A. Round robin reading

   B. Read aloud/think aloud

   C. Silent sustained reading

   D. Popcorn reading

11. Which of the following is NOT a comprehension skill?

    A. Main idea

    B. Phonemic awareness

    C. Author's purpose

    D. Summarization

12. Students are recognizing spelling and pronunciation rules for the suffix -tion. What are students engaging in?

    A. Phonics

    B. Phonemic awareness

    C. Phonological awareness

    D. Semantic analysis

Use the following scenario to answer questions 13 and 14.

A teacher is working with students on words. She tells the students to say the word *hat*. They all say the word *hat*. Then she tells them to say the word hat with a /p/ sound in the beginning instead of the /h/ sound.

13. The teacher is working on which skill with students?

    A. Phonics

    B. Fluency

    C. Comprehension

    D. Phonemic awareness

14. What strategy is the teacher using?

    A. Substitution

    B. Deletion

    C. Segmenting

    D. Isolation

15. Which of the following is a CVCC word?

    A. Make

    B. Pat

    C. Tack

    D. Shake

16. Students are deciding whether to write a persuasive essay or an expository essay. What should students consider first?

    A. Audience

    B. Length

    C. Publication

    D. Genre

17. What stage of writing are students in when they are writing down ideas and researching topics?

    A. Pre-writing

    B. Workshopping

    C. Editing

    D. Revising

18. Read the following paragraph and determine the text structure.

    A powerful tornado appeared out of nowhere. It was a tri-state tornado with high winds going about 200 mph. The people in the town were terrified because they had never seen a tornado of that size. Over 200 homes were destroyed that day.

    A. Problem and solution

    B. Chronological and sequential

    C. Descriptive

    D. Cause and effect

19. A student is writing words, reproduced below. The student is using what type of writing?

    # We went to the uther gas stashun.

    A. Conventional spelling

    B. Mock letters

    C. Inventive spelling

    D. Fluent writing

20. Which of the following would be the most appropriate example of persuasive writing?

    A. As she walked through the room, she remembered her childhood and was transported back in time.

    B. Picturesque mountains and pristine grass are the backdrop to the beautiful 19th century campus.

    C. In 1969, the United States made it to the moon, making the U.S. the most powerful nation in the world.

    D. This is the most pressing issue of our time, and young people should get out and vote.

21. Match the stage of writing to the activity.

1.	writing strings of words
2.	writing his or her name
3.	scribbling in a pattern
4.	scribbling randomly

A.	preliterate
B.	emergent
C.	transitional
D.	fluent

22. Free writing and drafting should be:

    A. Solitary and structured

    B. Exploratory and unstructured

    C. Conducted in structured whole groups

    D. Conducted in structured small groups

23. A teacher wants students to write a paragraph about their experience on the playground. Which of the following modes of writing will be most appropriate?

    A. Argumentative

    B. Narrative

    C. Informative

    D. Descriptive

24. A teacher is showing students how to use conjunctions. Which sentence would be most appropriate for this activity?

    A. Hey! How are you?

    B. She went to the store to buy candy.

    C. She was going home but first needed to help clean up.

    D. I ate my lunch very quickly yesterday.

25. Which of the following instructional methods helps students to avoid plagiarism?

    A. Showing students how to summarize information

    B. Using the copy paste shortcut

    C. Working in cooperative groups

    D. Using software to catch student who copy.

26. Classroom structures should include _____ to allow for multiple speaking and listening opportunities.

    A. Whole group lessons combined with small-group lessons

    B. Formal cooperative learning groups only

    C. Informal cooperative learning groups only

    D. A combination of independent and group work

27. Which of the following is the most effective way to help students find reliable resources for a research project?

   A. Teach students to only use blogs written by reputable people.

   B. Teach students how to find information in peer-reviewed academic journals.

   C. Show students how to use newspaper articles that match the topic being discussed.

   D. Only let students use the Internet to search *.gov* Internet sites.

28. Which of the following is considered a primary resource?

   A. Diary

   B. Newspaper article

   C. Textbook

   D. Biography

29. Which of the following is NOT a component of active listening?

   A. Paraphrasing what the speaker said

   B. Making eye contact

   C. Asking clarifying questions

   D. Using a recorder to document what is being said.

30. The following sentence is what type of sentence.

   I went to the store, and I bought a candy bar

   A. Simple sentence

   B. Complex sentence

   C. Compound sentence

   D. Compound Complex sentence

31. Which of the following would be the most appropriate first step when starting the writing process?

   A. Editing

   B. Peer review

   C. Revision

   D. Brainstorming

32. Which of the following would be most effective in developing phonemic awareness in students?

   A. Clapping words by their syllables.

   B. Using a spelling test.

   C. Diagraming sentences

   D. Singing songs with rhyming words.

33. A student sees the picture below writes:

SN

What would be the most appropriate next step in the spelling continuum?

A. Print using lowercase letters

B. Being to use medial vowel sounds

C. Blend consonant sounds

D. Recognize common sight words

34. A kindergarten teacher uses a large book in the front of the room and asks students, "Where should I begin reading this text?" The students point to the top left corner of the page. The teacher and students are working on:

A. Phonological awareness

B. Metacognition

C. Concepts of print

D. Prosody

35. Which of the following is considered environmental print?

A. Textbook

B. Essay

C. Street sign

D. Story book

36. When should students be given the opportunity to write?

A. When they can spell their name.

B. When they can hold a crayon or pencil.

C. When they understand phonological awareness.

D. When they get to kindergarten.

37. A teacher has several paper plates with dots to represent numbers. She shows a plate to a student who quickly and accurately identifies how many dots are on the paper plate. Which of the following describes the process the student is displaying?

A. Transitivity

B. Cognitive complexity

C. Flexibility

D. Subitizing

38. A teacher gives her students the following problem.

   There are six coconuts on a palm tree in the front yard. There are two coconuts on a palm tree in the back yard. How many more coconuts are there on the palm tree in the front yard?

   Which of the following best describes the structure of this problem?

   A. Add to, change unknown

   B. Compare, difference unknown

   C. Take apart, addend unknown

   D. Put together, total unknown

39. A teacher is conducting a lesson on perimeter. Which one of the following manipulatives would NOT be a good choice for the teacher to use for teaching this particular lesson?

   A. Tiles

   B. Geoboard

   C. Pattern blocks

   D. Base ten blocks

40. Which of the following is a decomposition of $\frac{3}{4}$?

   A. $\frac{1}{4} + \frac{1}{4} + \frac{1}{4} = \frac{3}{4}$

   B. $\frac{3}{4} = 0.75 = 75\%$

   C. $\frac{1}{4} + \frac{3}{4} = \frac{4}{4} = 1$

   D. $\frac{1}{2} < \frac{3}{4}$

41. While completing an addition problem, the teacher is having students use snap cubes to find the sum. Which instructional approach is the teacher using?

   A. Abstract

   B. Fluency

   C. Concrete

   D. Representational

42. A kindergarten teacher is beginning a lesson on the attributes of two-dimensional figures. Which of the following would be an appropriate strategy for the teacher to use to begin the lesson?

   A. Use dot paper or a geoboard to explore attributes of figures.

   B. Make a table and list the attributes of two-dimensional figures.

   C. Use geometric formulas to determine the attributes of two-dimensional figures.

   D. Use base ten blocks to explore the attributes of two-dimensional figures.

43. Which of the following best depicts why $3 \times 5 = 15$?

A. ● ● ● ● ●
 ● ● ● ● ●
 ● ● ● ● ●

B. ● ● ● ●
 ● ● ● ●
 ● ● ● ●

C. ● ● ● ●
 ● ● ● ●
 ● ● ● ●
 ● ● ● ●

D. ● ● ●
 ● ● ●
 ● ● ●
 ● ● ●
 ● ● ●

44. A teacher asks the class to mentally add 97 and 54. Miguel rethinks the problem as the following. Which of the following inventive mental strategy did Miguel use?

$$97 + 3 = 100$$
$$54 - 3 = 51$$
$$100 + 51 = 151$$

A. Combining tens

B. Compensation

C. Total unknown

D. Regrouping

45. If the number of prizes a person can win at a raffle and the number of guests are inversely related, what would be a possible equation for the relationship between the number of prizes a person wins and the number of guests?

A. When the number of guests goes up 10, the number of possible raffle prizes won goes up 10.

B. When the number of possible raffle prizes won goes up 15, number of guests goes up 10.

C. When the number of possible raffle prizes won goes up 30, number of guests goes down 20.

D. When the number of guests goes down 10, the number of possible raffle prizes won goes down 15.

46. Which of the following represents $-1\dfrac{3}{4}$ on the number line?

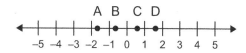

47. If $m = n$ and $n = p$, then $m = p$ is an example of what property?

A. Commutative property

B. Reflexive property

C. Symmetric property

D. Transitive property

48. A 3rd grade teacher asks the students to look at the picture below and answer the question. What is the teacher focusing on?

Who gets the bigger piece of pizza, student A with $\frac{1}{2}$ or student B with $\frac{2}{4}$?

Student A   Student B

A. Factoring

B. Equivalent fractions

C. Base ten comparison

D. Distribution

49. A 3rd grade teacher asks the students to look at the picture below and answer the question. What is the teacher demonstrating?

Student A   Student B

A. Fractions are parts of a whole.

B. Fraction comparisons are only valid when fractions refer to the same whole.

C. Fraction comparisons are valid regardless of the whole.

D. The same fraction can be represented a variety of ways.

50. A teacher has prekindergarten students put all the red blocks in one basket and all the blue blocks in another basket. The teacher is working with students on what skill?

A. Counting

B. Classifying

C. Comparing

D. Patterning

51. Students are learning about measurement. The teacher asks students to select the most appropriate metric measure for the classroom door. Which of the following students is correct?

A. Foot

B. Kilometer

C. Meter

D. Liter

52. A teacher is asking students to write down which TV show they like best out of 5 TV shows. She later shows them how this can be turned into percentages and organized in a chart. What type of data display would be most appropriate for this data?

    A. Bar graph

    B. Pictograph

    C. Line graph

    D. Pie chart

53. Which of the following represents the shaded region below?

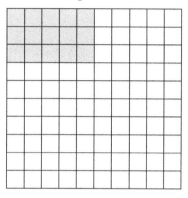

    A. 10% or 0.10

    B. 15% or 1.5

    C. 25% or 0.25

    D. 15% or 0.15

54. Which of the following properties of integers is represented by the numbers below?

    $-5 + 5 = 0$

    $+5 - 5 = 0$

    A. Inverse property of addition

    B. Distributive property

    C. Communitive property

    D. Reflexive property

55. Which of the following properties of integers is represented by the numbers below?

    $5 + 7 = 12$

    $7 + 5 = 12$

    A. Inverse property of addition

    B. Distributive property

    C. Communitive property

    D. Reflexive property

56. Which of the following is a possible net for a cube?

A.

C.

B.

D.

57. A rectangular backyard is fenced in using 200 feet of fencing. All sides are fenced except the side against the house. If the width of the house is 80 feet, how long is the backyard?

   A. 32 feet

   B. 60 feet

   C. 120 feet

   D. 160 feet

58. How many mini-4-ounce bags of snack mix can you make from a large 3.5 pound of snack mix?

   A. 16

   B. 14

   C. 13

   D. 12

59. A family wants to sod their 10 ft. by 50 ft. lawn, which is in the shape of a rectangle. If sod costs $3.00 per 10 ft^2, how much will it cost the family to sod their entire lawn?

   A. $50.00

   B. $1,500.00

   C. $150.00

   D. $300.00

60. Maria is replacing the carpet in her 10-foot by 15-foot living room. If the carpet she chose costs $4.00 per square foot, how much will it cost to replace the carpet?

   A. $150

   B. $400

   C. $450

   D. $600

61. Which of the following points on a number line has the greatest distance from $\frac{2}{3}$?

A. -2

B. 0

C. 1

D. 2

62. Which of the following manipulatives would be most effective in helping students understand positive and negative numbers?

A. Base ten blocks

B. Geoboard

C. Dice

D. Tiles

63. The teacher asks students to represent the following sentence with a number sentence.

There are 15 students total in our class. Some are absent today. There are 12 students in class today.

Student A: $15 - s = 12$

Student B: $s + 12 = 15$

Student C: $15 - \blacksquare = 12$

Student D: $\blacksquare + 12 = 15$

What are the students representing with the symbols or letters in the above number sentences?

A. A factor

B. A variable

C. A product

D. A sum

64. Students are working in pairs using flashcards to memorize addition math facts. The students are working on what math skill?

A. Abstract

B. Concrete

C. Fluency

D. Representational

65. A 2nd grade teacher is beginning a lesson on multiplication. What prerequisite skill is most important for students to understand multiplication?

A. Addition

B. Subtraction

C. Division

D. Place value

66. Which of the figures has 5 faces and 6 vertices?

    A. Triangular pyramid

    B. Triangular prism

    C. Rectangular prism

    D. Cylinder

67. A kindergarten teacher facilitates a learning project where students work together to design and create a pirate ship with recycled materials. Through her instructional design, what cognitive process is the teacher expecting students to use to complete the task?

    A. inductive reasoning

    B. creative thinking

    C. recall

    D. memory

68. Which of the following activities would be most effective in helping students sequence events in a story about Abraham Lincoln?

    A. Map

    B. Chart

    C. Timeline

    D. Journal

69. Which of the following activities would be most effective in helping students understand interdependence of living things and the environment?

    A. A teacher reads a story about people in two small villages who work together to protect the river from pollution because they use the river to fish for food and supply fresh water to the villages.

    B. Students work in groups to color pictures of rivers, houses, people, and other elements of village life.

    C. The teacher has a guest speaker come in and talk to students about a remote village in Africa that has no modern technology available.

    D. The teacher has students look up the word interdependence in the dictionary and they share out how that may work in todays society.

70. What would be the best way to teach third grade students about the Battle of Bunker Hill?

    A. Write a newspaper article about the Battle of Bunker Hill.

    B. Read the chapter in the textbook on the Battle of Bunker Hill and answer questions at the end.

    C. Look at a map and identify where the Battle of Bunker Hill took place.

    D. Coordinate in groups to research the battle and then role-play what they have discovered.

71. A group of 2nd grade students is having a difficult time understanding how time zones work. Which of the following activities would help to show students why time is different in other parts of the world?

    A. Use a map and describe how time zones work with lines of longitude and then have students discuss in groups.

    B. Use a globe and a flashlight to show when it is daylight in some parts of the world it is night in other parts of the world.

    C. Read a story about times zones to the class and encourage students to ask questions about the story.

    D. Show a video about time zones and how activities in different cities around the world are taking place at different times.

72. Which of the following teaching approaches demonstrates cultural responsiveness when presenting historical events that are negative for the dominant culture?

    A. Paraphrase the material to avoid uncomfortable discussion.

    B. Focus on the events that are positive for the dominant culture.

    C. Choose culturally relevant material that is aligned to state standards.

    D. Ask parents for permission to discuss certain historical events with their students.

73. Mr. Lopez wants to explain the sophistication of the Mayan civilization. What would be the best way to engage students?

    A. Have a guest speaker come in and talk about the Ancient Mayans.

    B. Look at a map to discover where the Mayan civilization was located.

    C. Read about the Mayans in a textbook.

    D. Take a virtual tour on the Internet of Mayan temples and artifacts.

74. Which of the following is described as a community with high population density and usually associated with a city?

    A. Rural

    B. Urban

    C. Country

    D. Region

75. Ms. Green is explaining relative location to her 1st grade students. Which of the following would be the best activity to help reinforce this concept?

    A. Have students look up the longitude and latitude coordinates for the school.

    B. Ask students to explain to their partners how to get to school from the nearby park.

    C. Have students locate the school on an online map.

    D. Have students determine whether the school is in an urban area or rural area.

76. Students are working in groups to discuss the different celebrations they participate in for the holidays. Some participate in Hannukah. Others participate in Christmas. Which of the following activities would help students meet the objective below?

The students will understand unity and diversity within and across groups?

A. Have students discuss the different traditions they participate in and then find ways in which they are similar (food, music, family, etc.).

B. Have students read about the importance of tolerance of other peoples' traditions during the holiday season.

C. Have students interview their family members about the different celebrations they participate in and the discuss in their cooperative groups.

D. Have students read about different cultural celebrations around the world and discuss similarities and difference as a class.

77. The _____ is a line that runs between Russia and Alaska and goes around political boundaries in the Pacific Ocean.

A. Prime Meridian

B. International Date Line

C. Equator

D. Latitude and longitude

78. A student is working on an assignment in social studies class. The student is determined to finish the assignment before the end of class. This will bring a sense of accomplishment to the student. This is an example of:

A. Self-regulation

B. Self-awareness

C. Self-evaluation

D. Self-efficacy

79. Students are working in groups to learn about the 3 branches of government. Students are talking about how Congress makes laws. Which branch of government are the students working on?

A. Senate

B. Executive

C. Legislative

D. Judicial

80. Which of the following would be considered a region?

A. Southwest United States

B. Africa

C. Wisconsin

D. The Equator

81. Which of the following would be an example of geography?

    A. Understanding that there are 7 continents in the world.

    B. Understanding that humans interact with their environment.

    C. Understanding that different societies have different traditions.

    D. Understanding that cultures are similar in many ways.

82. Which of the following activities would be most effective in discussing causes and solutions to human made pollution?

    A. Debate

    B. Direct instruction

    C. Direct intervention

    D. Cooperative learning

83. A 1st grade teacher is showing students how the earth is divided into 4 quadrants—north, south, east, and west. Choose all of the concepts the students are learning about in this lesson.

    A. The equator

    B. The international dateline

    C. The hemispheres

    D. The prime meridian

84. Which would be the best way to activate students' curiosity of the world around them?

    A. Have students go outside and identify as many living and nonliving things as they can.

    B. Have students draw as many living and nonliving things as they can.

    C. Have students compete to see how many living and nonliving things they can identify.

    D. Have students research on the computer living and nonliving things.

85. What would be the best way for a teacher to assess how students apply the scientific method?

    A. Formatively assess students by walking around the lab and watch how students apply the scientific method.

    B. Use a teacher-made multiple-choice assessment with scientific method questions.

    C. Administer a state-mandated assessment that assesses the standards for scientific method.

    D. Survey students to identify their understanding of the scientific method.

86. Which of the following activities would be most effective in helping students understand how parts of a flower work?

    A. Read about flowers in the textbook.

    B. Look at a diagram of a flower.

    C. Dissect a flower and examine its organs.

    D. Draw a flower and label its reproductive organs.

87. Ms. Francis wants to conduct a lab with her students. What is the best way to ensure safety, efficiency, and student learning?

   A. Get students into groups to learn on their own.

   B. Predetermine groups, conduct the lab, and debrief.

   C. Predetermine groups, assign specific roles for each student, and practice procedures.

   D. Go over the scientific method to ensure students understand the process of the lab.

88. Metals are good _____ in that electric current can flow freely down/through them.

   A. insulators

   B. components

   C. contractors

   D. conductors

89. In a magnet, opposite sides _____ and same sides _____.

   A. attract, attract

   B. repel, attract

   C. attract, repel

   D. repel, repel

90. A rock sitting on top of a hill has what kind of energy?

   A. Kinetic

   B. Mechanical

   C. Chemical

   D. Potential

91. When you push a box through the doorway, you are using:

   A. Chemical energy

   B. Kinetic energy

   C. Mechanical energy

   D. Potential energy

92. A river flows through a canyon and picks up silt. That sediment and silt runs downstream and deposits where the river ends. When that material gets to the beach, it sits there. Over millions of years, _____ form.

   A. Fossils

   B. Sedimentary rocks

   C. Igneous rocks

   D. Metamorphic rocks

93. Mr. Lopez is teaching a unit on seasons. He explains why summer days are longer and winter days are shorter. What should Mr. Lopez emphasize regarding the Earth when explaining this phenomenon?

    A. Revolution around the sun

    B. Tilt on its axis

    C. Position in the solar system

    D. Distance away from the sun

94. What are the main differences between plant and animal cells? Choose all that apply.

    A. Animal cells have a cell wall, and plant cells have a cell membrane.

    B. Plant cells have a cell wall, and animal cells have a cell membrane.

    C. Animal cells have mitochondria, and plant cells have a nucleus.

    D. Plant cells go through photosynthesis while animal cells go through cellular respiration.

95. Ms. Smith is teaching her students that cells divide to make other cells. Ms. Smith is teaching:

    A. Evolution

    B. Natural selection

    C. Cell theory

    D. Classification

96. This animal has an open circulatory system:

    A. Grasshopper

    B. Cow

    C. Fish

    D. Snake

97. Which of the following would be most effective when describing an abstract concept like the solar system or an animal cell to first grade students?

    A. Use a model

    B. Use a graph

    C. Use the textbook

    D. Use direct instruction

98. A teacher is planning a unit on heredity. At the end of the unit, she wants to help students apply their knowledge by engaging in a lab. However, the school does not have the resources for the lab she wants to administer. What would be the best way to help students in this situation?

    A. Have students work in cooperative groups to discuss the concepts of the lesson and answer comprehension questions.

    B. Have students engage with a virtual lab that covers the same learning objectives and standards that the traditional lab would.

    C. Have a guest speaker come in and present the lab information in an engaging and thoughtful way and have students take notes in their lab journals.

    D. Have students do the lab at home by providing parents with the information and have students respond in writing what they found.

99. What can an early childhood teacher do to increase awareness about research in science education and practices that help increase science achievement in young children?

  A. Survey parents to see what they think their students need in the science classroom.

  B. Join the National Science Teacher Association and subscribe to their information.

  C. Work with a peer teacher on her science instruction and classroom management.

  D. Use social media to connect with other science teachers and share information.

100. Which of the following would be most effective in engaging English language learners (ELLs) in science instruction?

  A. Ask another student to translate the information to the ELLs.

  B. Send home the science information to the students' parents.

  C. Ask for a paraprofessional (translator) to help during that class period.

  D. Provide the science materials in the students' home languages.

101. A preschool teacher is helping students develop their gross motor skills. Which of the following would be most effective?

  A. Handwriting exercises

  B. Finger painting

  C. Dancing

  D. Keyboarding skills

102. Which of the following activities is most effective in helping 2-year-old students develop their curiosity and imagination?

  A. Write essays

  B. Pretend play

  C. Cooperative learning

  D. Direct instruction

103. According to the US Department of Agriculture's MyPlate, children 2-3 years old should have how many cups of veggies a day?

  A. 1 cup

  B. 3 cups

  C. 6 cups

  D. 8 cups

104. Which of the following are the most important sources of fiber, potassium, folic acid, vitamin A and vitamin B?

  A. Fruits

  B. Vegetables

  C. Meat

  D. Fats

105. Which of the following would be the most appropriate places for a teacher to find resources to help plan lessons about health and diet?

A. A health blog

B. An exercise YouTube channel

C. U.S. Dietary Guidelines for Americans

D. A Cookbook

106. Which of the following food groups should take up the most room on a child's plate, according to the US Department of Agriculture's MyPlate?

A. Fats

B. Dairy

C. Fruits

D. Vegetables

107. A first-grade teacher is trying to get students to focus on their math after they return from lunch. Which of the following would be most effective?

A. Consequences for disruptive behavior

B. Rewards for paying attention and finishing work

C. Providing students with naptime after lunch

D. Letting students take short brain breaks to get up and move their bodies.

108. Which of the following would be the best resources for students who are making an original piece of art?

A. Digital camera

B. Photos from magazines

C. Different colored clay

D. Newspaper

109. Which of the following is a prerequisite skill for skipping?

A. Hopping

B. Running

C. Walking

D. Spinning

110. Which of the following situations requires a student to have agility?

A. Catching a ball thrown unexpectedly

B. Sprinting in a race

C. Dribbling a basketball

D. Changing course while running

111. Which of the following would do the most to increase cardiovascular health?

    A. Running

    B. Lifting weights

    C. Eating healthy

    D. Getting enough sleep

112. A teacher is working with students using complex text. Which of the following would be most effective in helping students understand the meaning of complex text?

    A. Have students work in cooperative groups to fill out a worksheet about the story.

    B. Have students engage in either sculpting, painting, or drawing main characters, scenes, and plot of the story.

    C. Have students find relevant vocabulary in the text and look those words up in the dictionary.

    D. Have students find pictures in a magazine that represent the story.

113. Students are learning about the color wheel. They are learning that there are three primary colors and all other colors come from mixing those three colors. The three primary colors are:

    A. Green, purple, red

    B. Red, blue, yellow

    C. Red, blue, green

    D. Orange, blue, purple

114. Students are singing a song in class, but the teacher wants them to increase the pace they are singing. She is asking them to increase the:

    A. Pitch

    B. Harmony

    C. Tempo

    D. Melody

115. Prekindergarten students are working on important elements of dental health. The teacher is using a model of a set of teeth to explain these concepts. Which of the following would be most developmentally appropriate and effective in teaching students about dental health?

    A. Show the students how molars work with other teeth to break down food.

    B. Describe the evolutionary reason for molars.

    C. Explain how most people will have their wisdom teeth removed at some point.

    D. Show students how to brush their teeth and how to reach the molars with a toothbrush.

116. First-grade students are learning about how people in other parts of the world build their homes from adobe or a heavy clay soil used to make sun-dried bricks. What would be the most effective activity to include in this lesson?

    A. Students look at pictures of adobe houses and use clay to make miniature adobe houses.

    B. A guest speaker, who builds adobe houses, comes in to describe the building process to students.

    C. Students look up information about adobe houses on the Internet and share what they find.

    D. Students work in cooperative groups to read about adobe and discuss what they've learned.

117. When working with students on art projects where there are lots of materials being used, what should the teacher be sure to do?

    A. Set rewards for cleaning up when it's time.

    B. Communicate consequences for not respecting the supplies or overusing supplies.

    C. Communicate clear expectations and practice procedures regularly for materials use and clean-up.

    D. Send home information to parents, so they understand the expectations and procedures.

118. Helping students understand teamwork and how it contributes to the fun of sports and activities is part of which domain?

    A. Cognitive

    B. Psychomotor

    C. Affective

    D. Personal

119. Which of the following is most important when teaching students about staying healthy and preventing disease?

    A. Making sure they understand where viruses come from and how they can be prevented.

    B. Making sure they understand that regular doctor's visits are essential in staying healthy.

    C. Making sure they understand that eating healthy is a way to prevent disease.

    D. Making sure they understand the proper way to wash their hands and do it regularly.

120. Which of the following is most effective when teaching students good sportsmanship during PE class?

    A. Show a video of great teams that show good sportsmanship.

    B. Read an excerpt from a famous athlete's memoir about sportsmanship.

    C. Reward students for showing good sportsmanship, so others do it too.

    D. Model good sportsmanship and recognize good sportsmanship when it happens.

This page intentionally left blank.

Answers and Explanations

Number	Answer	Section	Explanation
1	A	Language and Literacy	All of the individual skills mentioned in the question fit under the umbrella of phonological awareness. Phonological awareness is a broad set of skills that includes identifying and manipulating units of oral language—parts such as phonemes in words, syllables, and onsets and rimes. Students with phonological awareness also understand conventional spelling. Remember, phonemic awareness is a sub-skill of phonological awareness and only deals with the smallest unit of sound—the phoneme. Signs of strong phonemic awareness include being able to hear rhyme and alliteration. Although they are often used interchangeably, when talking about reading skills, phonological awareness is usually the correct term.
2	C	Language and Literacy	Phonemic awareness is understanding the individual sounds—or phonemes—in words. When you see the word *phonemic*, think of the root word *phone*, which is related to sound. Answers A, B, and D all reference words and spelling, which is connected to phonics not phonemic awareness.
3	D	Language and Literacy	Morphology is the study of the structure of words. Using prefixes, roots and suffixes is a way to use morphology. The only answer choice that uses prefixes, roots, and suffixes is answer D.
4	C	Language and Literacy	When teaching vocabulary, students must have the opportunity to interact with words in an authentic manner. Answer A is a best practice because using context clues allows the students to figure out new vocabulary by evaluating words and ideas around the vocabulary words. Answer B is also a best practice because analyzing prefixes, suffixes, and roots is a way to deconstruct a word by understanding its word parts. Answer D is also a best practice because word walls are interactive. Out of all the answers, answer C is *not* the best practice. Dictionaries are amazing tools to use as a supplement to instruction. However, explicitly using a dictionary is not an authentic practice in vocabulary instruction.
5	C	Language and Literacy	Sematic cueing system is using meaning to understand. Therefore, the question, "Does that make sense?" is the most appropriate here. Answer A has to do with a syntactic cueing system. Answers B and D are letter-sound relationships, which is graphophonic cueing system.
6	A	Language and Literacy	Because no letters or words are used and students are using the picture to say the word *bug*, the students are in the pre-alphabetic stage (before letter stage).
7	D	Language and Literacy	Etymology is the study of the origin of words and the way in which their meanings have changed throughout history. *Prescription, transcript,* and *manuscript* all have the Latin root word *script,* which means *written.*

Number	Answer	Section	Explanation
8	A	Language and Literacy	Students are sharing in the reading process. Therefore, this is shared reading. Choral reading is reading in unison, repeated reading is reading a passage again and again for fluency. Round Robin reading is having students read aloud. Round robin reading is usually not the correct answer on this exam.
9	C	Language and Literacy	Sight words are words students memorize. They are words like *the, what, why, said*, etc. It is most effective for students to memorize these words because these words appear so frequently in text.
10	B	Language and Literacy	Metacognition is thinking about thinking. In a read aloud/think aloud activity, the teacher models the process of thinking while reading the text aloud to students. In addition, cognition is thinking. Answer B has the word *think* in it.
11	B	Language and Literacy	Phonemic awareness is an emergent reading skill. Comprehension is a higher-order skill that comes after phonemic awareness. Answers A, B and D are all associated with comprehension.
12	A	Language and Literacy	Phonics is letter/sound relationships. In this example, students are seeing the letter combination *tion*. They learn that *tion* makes a *shun* sound.
13	D	Language and Literacy	The teacher is focusing solely on the sounds in words. There is no writing or reading, so you can eliminate answers A, B, and C.
14	A	Language and Literacy	The key words in the question stem are *instead of*. That indicates the teacher and students are replacing or substituting one sound for another in a word. Substitution is a phonemic awareness activity.
15	C	Language and Literacy	CVCC is consonant, vowel, consonant, consonant. The only answer choices that follow that pattern is answer C—*tack*.
16	A	Language and Literacy	One of the most important components of writing is the ability to adapt communication in relation to audience, task, purpose, and discipline. Length, publication and genre are not important considerations.
17	A	Language and Literacy	This is the before writing stage where students generate ideas. Answers B, C, and D all come after the pre-writing stage.
18	D	Language and Literacy	This is an example of the tornado (cause) impacting a town and homes (effect). No solutions are discussed, which eliminates answer A. The passage is not in chronological order. Finally, while there is some description of the tornado, cause and effect fits better than description.
19	C	Language and Literacy	The student is spelling phonetically (using sounds in the words). This is called inventive spelling and is an essential part of developing writing skills.

Number	Answer	Section	Explanation
20	D	Language and Literacy	Answer A is a narrative. Answer B is descriptive. Answer C is informational. Answer D is persuasive. The words "most pressing issue of our time" are claim-based and persuasive.
21	1-D 2-C 3-B 4-A	Language and Literacy	D. **Fluent.** Conventional spelling. C. **Transitional.** Conventional letters and inventive spelling. B. **Emergent.** Mock handwriting and mock letters. A. **Preliterate.** Random marks or scribbles.
22	B	Language and Literacy	Free writing and drafting should be unstructured where students have the opportunity to explore ideas and get those ideas down on paper. Free writing is being free to write anything. It is an essential part of the writing process.
23	B	Language and Literacy	The key words in the question stem are *about their experience.* Narrative essays are first-person accounts about a personal experience.
24	C	Language and Literacy	A conjunction is one of the following: for, and, nor, but, or, yet, so. You can remember this by the acronym FANBOYS.
25	A	Language and Literacy	Answer A is the only practice that helps students avoid plagiarism. Using the copy paste tool increases the likelihood students will plagiarize. Working in cooperative groups and using plagiarism software does not prevent students from plagiarizing.
26	A	Language and Literacy	A combination of whole-group and small-group activities allows for students to both listen (whole group) and speak (small group). The word *multiple* is key. Answers B and C both have the qualifier—*only*—so eliminate those. Independent work does not allow for speaking and listening, so D can also be eliminated.
27	B	Language and Literacy	When looking for relevant and scholarly resources for research, peer-reviewed, academic journals are the most reliable place. The information in these journals are scholarly and reviewed. Early in their academic careers, students should be taught how to navigate these journals.
28	A	Language and Literacy	Primary resources are original sources, and a diary is an original source. Answers B, C and D are all secondary sources.
29	D	Language and Literacy	While a recording device is a useful tool in documenting what a speaker says, it is not necessarily part of the active listening process. A student could push record on the recorder and then stop listening to what is being said. Answers A, B, and C are all components of active listening.

Number	Answer	Section	Explanation
30	C	Language and Literacy	This sentence has two independent clauses joined by a comma and conjunction, which makes it a compound sentence.
31	D	Language and Literacy	Brainstorming is considered part of the prewriting process. Therefore, it is the best answer.
32	D	Language and Literacy	Rhyme goes with phonemic awareness because rhyme has to do with sounds in words. Phonemic awareness focuses on the individual sounds in words.
33	B	Language and Literacy	Students spell with consonants first. In this case, the student spells *sun* as *SN*. Then they will start to use medial vowel sounds. In this case the medial vowel sound is the /u/. That would be the next step for the student.
34	C	Language and Literacy	Understanding that we read from left to right, top to bottom is a concept of print.
35	C	Language and Literacy	Signs, labels and other writing that is part of our daily lives are considered types of environmental print. Students will begin to understand the symbols with the words. For example, students might say, "Stop!" when they see a stop sign. This is an example of environmental print.
36	B	Language and Literacy	As soon as students can hold a pencil or crayon, they should be given the opportunity to write. It is never too early. Let students scribble, use mock letters, and try to spell. This will lead to progress in the skill.
37	D	Math	When a student can identify the number of items in a group without having to count them, this is known as subitizing.
38	B	Math	This is a subtraction problem where you are comparing two values with the difference between them unknown.
39	D	Math	Base ten blocks would NOT be the best choice for teaching perimeter because they do not change in dimension, and they are used for place value. Tiles can be organized in an array to show area. Geoboards are pegs on a board that show attributes of geometric shapes, which would help with area. Pattern blocks can also be used to show area.
40	A	Math	The correct answer choice is A because decomposing a fraction means to break a fraction up into the sum of smaller parts with the same denominator. Options B, C, and D do not break the fraction into smaller parts.
41	C	Math	Using a hands-on approach to learning is part of the CRA model (concrete-representational-abstract) and is a concrete approach.

Number	Answer	Section	Explanation
42	A	Math	To begin any lesson, a teacher should start at the concrete, hands-on phase of student learning before moving on to more abstract definitions and facts. A geoboard is a way for students to understand shapes in a concrete manner. All of the other answer choices are representational or abstract. Remember the CRA model.
43	A	Math	The concrete representation of the multiplication problem is a picture or array of 3 groups of 5 items. The array in option A contains 3 rows, each with 5 dots.
44	B	Math	Miguel rewrote the first number to something easier to work with, which is compensation—borrowing pieces of one number to compensate for another to make the problem easier to solve.
45	C	Math	Inversely related means when one value goes up, the other value goes down. The numbers in the answer choices do not matter. Just choose the answer where one goes up and the other goes down.
46	A	Math	The point $-1\frac{3}{4}$ is between -1 and -2 on the number line, so point A is the correct answer choice.
47	D	Math	This is an example of the transitive property. See table on page 75-76.
48	B	Math	The teacher is demonstrating that $\frac{1}{2}$ is equal or equivalent to $\frac{2}{4}$. This is equivalent fractions.
49	B	Math	The teacher is dividing two different shapes to show that fraction comparisons are only valid if you are working with the same whole. Both of these objects represent $\frac{1}{2}$. However, $\frac{1}{2}$ of the circle is not the same as $\frac{1}{2}$ of the rectangle.
50	B	Math	Students are organizing the blocks by color, which is classifying.
51	C	Math	A meter is roughly 3 feet. Therefore, a meter is the most appropriate measure for a classroom door. The teacher asks for the metric measure, so answer A, foot, is not correct. A kilometer is too big, eliminating answer B. Finally, a liter is used to measure liquid not distance.
52	D	Math	A pie chart is a visual representation that best shows proportional relationships. The data is presented in percentages and compares parts to a whole. In this case, the teacher is displaying the percentages of the whole class in relation to their favorite tv shows. A pie chart or circle graph is the best choice for this.

Number	Answer	Section	Explanation
53	D	Math	15 of the 100 squares are shaded, so this represents 15%. To change 15% to a decimal, move the decimal point two places to the left. 15% = 0.15.
54	A	Math	The inverse property of addition is adding a number and its opposite resulting in a sum equal to 0. That is what is displayed in the example.
55	C	Math	The commutative property of addition means that the order in which the addends are added results in the same sum. A + B = C is the same as B + A = C.
56	B	Math	The net of a cube should have 4 squares in a row and squares that are able to be folded to create the top and bottom. Answer choice A does not have enough squares to create a cube, and answer choice D does not have 4 squares in a row to create the sides. Answer choice C needs the squares on the sides to be on opposite sides so one covers the top and the other covers the bottom.
57	B	Math	Even though the question says the backyard is a rectangle, you are only trying to find 3 sides of the fence. The 4th side is the house and does not need to be fenced. This means the 3 remaining sides of the fence must add up to 200 feet. Since the house represents the width of the fence, then the side opposite of the house is also 80 feet. Next you have to figure out the length. With a total of 200 feet of fencing, subtract 80 feet (the side opposite of the house) to get 120 feet (the remaining amount of fence). 200 − 80 = 120 Next, divide 120 by 2 since opposite sides of rectangles are the same length. 120 ÷ 2 = 60
58	B	Math	Because 1 pound = 16 ounces, you can make four 4-ounce bags for each pound and two 4-ounce bags for each half pound. Thus for 3.5 pounds you can make 12 + 2 = 14 mini bags.
59	C	Math	Find the area of the rectangular lawn. $10 \cdot 50 = 500 \text{ ft}^2$ Sod costs $3.00 per 10 ft², so divide 500 by 10 to get the number of 10 ft² parcels of sod needed. 500 ÷ 10 = 50 Last, multiply 50 by $3.00 to get the cost of sodding the entire yard. $50 \cdot \$3 = \$150$

Number	Answer	Section	Explanation
60	D	Math	Find the area of the room first. 10 x 15 = 150. Then multiply that by $4.00 and you will get $600.
61	A	Math	$\frac{2}{3}$ on a number line is in between 0 and 1. Therefore, –2 is the furthest away from $\frac{2}{3}$.
62	D	Math	Tiles are the most useful in this situation. The teacher can use green tiles to represent positive numbers and red tiles to represent negative numbers. The teacher can show that if there are more negative tiles than positive, then the number is negative.
63	B	Math	The variable is an unknown. In this case, students use ■ or s to represent the unknown or variable.
64	C	Math	Memorization of math facts helps with math fluency, specifically automaticity. Like memorizing sight words, memorizing math facts helps students build automatic skills useful in solving complex math problems.
65	A	Math	Multiplication is repeated addition. Therefore, answer A is the best answer choice.
66	B	Math	The faces of a three-dimensional figure are the sides and the vertices are the points where the edges of each side meet. The correct answer choice here is triangular prism.
67	B	Social Studies	Key words from the scenario are *design* and *create* because these are mentioned in the definition of creative thinking. While the children will use a variety of thinking skills to collaboratively design and create their pirate ships creative thinking is the dominant cognitive thinking process from this list.
68	C	Social Studies	The key word in this question is sequence, and a timeline would be most effective in this situation.
69	A	Social Studies	Answer A is the only choice that outlines interdependence—the dependence of two or more people or things on each other.
70	D	Social Studies	Answer D incorporates research and play. For early childhood students, and all students for that matter, play is essential in learning.

PRACTICE TEST

Number	Answer	Section	Explanation
71	B	Social Studies	Answer B is using a model to bring the abstract to the concrete. This method demonstrates how time zones work and is the best activity here.
72	C	Social Studies	It is important to choose materials that contain current, correct information and are aligned to the state-standards. It is also important not to gloss over or leave out information that is unfavorable to the dominant culture. If the material is standards-aligned, there is no need to request parents' permission.
73	D	Social Studies	A virtual tour would be a way for students to see the Mayan relics without having to actually travel. The other choices are not as effective as a virtual tour.
74	B	Social Studies	Urban communities are cities with high population density.
75	B	Social Studies	Relative location is a point in relation to another point. For example, the school is across the street from the park. The answer choice that supports this concept is B. Answer A and C work for absolute location. Answer D is not related to location.
76	A	Social Studies	Answer A is the best choice for 2 reasons: 1) it fulfils the objective of the lesson (unity and diversity), and 2) it uses relevance and real-world experience. Because students are discussing their own experiences, they are seeing how the objective applies to their lives. Answer choice D also achieves the objective, but answer A is most effective here because of the relevance to the students' lives.
77	B	Social Studies	The International Date Line (IDL) separates two consecutive calendar dates and is located in the Pacific Ocean. The IDL approximately follows the 180-degree longitudinal line east or west of the Prime Meridian and circumvents political boundaries.
78	D	Social Studies	A belief in one's own ability to do something, find resources, gain knowledge and problem-solve is the key to understanding one's self-efficacy.
79	C	Social Studies	Congress is part of the legislative branch. Congress is made up of two chambers: House of Representatives and Senate. The role of Congress is to create and pass laws.
80	A	Social Studies	Regions are areas broadly divided by physical characteristics, human impact characteristics, and the interaction of humanity and the environment. The southwest United States is a region. None of the other answer choices are regions.

Number	Answer	Section	Explanation
81	A	Social Studies	Answer A is the only choice that has to do with the world in special terms or geography. All the other choices are about anthropology or sociology.
82	D	Social Studies	The key word in the question is solution. The only activity that supports a solution is cooperative learning. Students can work together to come up with solutions to the pollution problem. Debates are to discuss different points of view. Direct instruction is when the teacher does most of the work in the front of the classroom. Direct intervention does not fit this situation.
83	A, C, & D	Social Studies	The students are learning about the hemispheres. They are also learning that the Prime Meridian and Equator divide the Earth into hemispheres. Therefore, A, C, and D are all correct. The international dateline is the only answer that does not fit.
84	A	Science	Getting students outside and interacting with the real world is an effective way to get students involved in science.
85	A	Science	A performance-based, formative assessment, in this case, observing students during a lab, is the best way to assess the skills in applying the scientific method.
86	C	Science	Hands-on, real-world activities are most effective when explaining science. Also, dissection is ideal when it is ethical and appropriate. It is appropriate and ethical for students to dissect a flower to learn about the sexual organs of the plant. This is the best choice.
87	C	Science	The best words in the answer choices are *practice procedures*, making answer C the best choice. Pre-determining groups is also helpful, so the teacher can control who is working with whom. Assigning specific roles is also effective, so each student understands exactly what to do. Remember, the word *procedures* is on the good words list.
88	D	Science	An electrical conductor is a substance in which electrical charges, usually electrons, move easily from atom to atom with the application of voltage. Metals are good conductors.
89	C	Science	A magnet's north pole is attracted to the south pole. Opposites attract and same sides repel.
90	D	Science	Potential energy is the energy stored in an object as the result of its vertical position or height.
91	C	Science	Mechanical energy is the sum of kinetic and potential energy on an object that is used to do work.

Number	Answer	Section	Explanation
92	B	Science	Sedimentation is the process that causes mineral and/or organic particles to settle in place and become sedimentary rocks.
93	B	Science	The seasons are the result of Earth, tilted on its axis, traveling around the sun. Summer happens in the hemisphere tilted toward the sun, and winter happens in the hemisphere tilted away from the sun.
94	B & D	Science	Both answer choices B and D are the main differences between plant and animal cells. That eliminates A because A is the opposite of the correct answer. Also, both plant and animal cells have a nucleus, eliminating C. Plant cell – cell wall Animal cell – plasma membrane Plant cell – photosynthesis Animal cell – cellular respiration
95	C	Science	Cell theory has three parts: all living things are made of cells; cells come from pre-existing cells (they divide); and cells are the basic unit of life.
96	A	Science	In an open circulatory system, blood and oxygen flow through open spaces within the animal. In a closed circulatory system, oxygen enters the body through lungs and gills. Invertebrates like grasshoppers have open circulatory systems. Vertebrates like fish, cows, and snakes have closed circulatory systems. This is another way to classify animals.
97	A	Science	Science teachers can use models to communicate ideas and to represent abstract phenomena. For this situation, using a model is most effective because it takes something abstract and brings it into the concrete.
98	B	Science	A virtual lab is the most effective answer choice here. Students can input data, gather information, and conduct an experiment in a virtual lab. Virtual labs are also most effective because they allow students the experience even if the resources are not available for the physical lab.
99	B	Science	The National Science Teacher Association and other associations like it have professional development opportunities, relevant research, standards and more for teachers of science. Teachers should consider joining organizations like these because it helps teachers to stay current and effective.

PRACTICE TEST

Number	Answer	Section	Explanation
100	D	Science	The best answer for this question is to provide the student with materials in his or her home language. A paraprofessional is helpful but asking the principal to provide a paraprofessional is usually the wrong answer. As the teacher, you have to figure out ways to engage different students.
101	C	PE & Art	Gross motor skills involve large muscles in the legs, arms and torso, making choice C the best answer. Answer A, B and D are all activities to develop fine motor skills, or the skills that involve the small muscles in the hands and fingers.
102	B	PE & Art	Pretend play is always a good answer on this exam because young children, and older children for that matter, learn through play. If you see play in an answer choice on this exam, it is most likely the answer. Play is very important, and teachers must make time for it throughout the day.
103	A	PE & Art	Children 2-3 years old should have 1 cup of vegetables per day. The largest amount of recommended vegetables is 3 cups per day for adult men.
104	B	PE & Art	Vegetables are the most important nutrient for fiber, potassium, and vitamin A and C.
105	C	PE & Art	This is the official United States website for dietary guidelines and the most reliable information for health and diet: https://www.dietaryguidelines.gov/.
106	D	PE & Art	According to the US Department of Agriculture's MyPlate, veggies are the largest portion of the plate along with protein.
107	D	PE & Art	Students will often need to get up and move their bodies in order to pay attention. Short brain breaks with movement is the most effective choice here. Eliminate all the negative answers and answers that have to do with external rewards.
108	C	PE & Art	To be developmentally appropriate, you would not give students a digital camera. Also, the question says, original art, which eliminates the newspaper and magazine pictures. That leaves clay as the best answer.
109	A	PE & Art	Before a student can learn to skip, the student must learn to hop. The other skills listed are not related to skipping.
110	D	PE & Art	Agility is the capacity to change course. A – reaction time B – speed C – coordination D – agility

Number	Answer	Section	Explanation
111	A	PE & Art	Running is an excellent means of conditioning the cardiovascular system. It is a highly aerobic activity that uses both fatty acids and carbohydrates for energy. While all of the choices result in health benefits, running is best for cardiovascular.
112	B	PE & Art	Answer choice B has all the good activities for artistic expression, which is essential in helping students understand complex concepts.
113	B	PE & Art	The three primary colors are red, blue, and yellow. All other colors, like green, purple and orange, come from mixing the primary colors.
114	C	PE & Art	The tempo is the rate of speed of a musical piece or passage indicated by one of a series of directions
115	D	PE & Art	Early childhood teachers must show students how to maintain good dental health. Describing molars and their functions is not as important as showing students how to brush their teeth effectively. Answer D is best here.
116	A	PE & Art	The best activity would be to use clay and build their own adobe houses. This is hands on, fun, and artistic. Finding information on the Internet and reading in cooperative groups is okay. However, these are 1st graders. Expressing what they've learned with clay is best. Remember, a guest speaker is the same as direct instruction. It can be very boring for students.
117	C	PE & Art	Setting clear expectations and practicing procedures are always on the top of the good words list when it comes to classroom practice. This answer choice is the most effective out of all the others.
118	C	PE & Art	The affective domain includes the feelings, emotions, and attitudes of the individual. This is the domain where PE teachers focus on teamwork, good sportsmanship, working together, and feeling good about exercise. Psychomotor is physical. Cognitive is about the brain and knowledge. Finally, there is no personal domain; that is a nonsense answer.
119	D	PE & Art	In the early grades, hand washing is the most important thing we can do to show students how to prevent disease. Early childhood students often forget to wash their hands. Therefore, explicit practice with handwashing is the best choice here.
120	D	PE & Art	The most powerful tool teachers have is their ability to model the type of behavior they want to see in the classroom. This is connected to social learning theory. Students do what they see the teacher do. Therefore, modeling positive behaviors will result in students exhibiting positive behaviors.

Bibliography

Agosto, D. E. (2002). *Criteria for evaluating multicultural literature.* Retrieved from http://www.pages.drexel.edu/~dea22/multicultural.html

Bandura, Alfred (1971). *Social learning theory.* General Learning Press, New York. Retrieved from http://www.asecib.ase.ro/mps/Bandura_SocialLearningTheory.pdf

Common Core State Standards (2019). English Language Arts Standards. Retrieved from http://www.corestandards.org/ELA-Literacy/introduction/students-who-are-college-and-career-ready-in-reading-writing-speaking-listening-language/

Educational Testing Services. (n.d.). *The Praxis Study Companion: Early Childhood 5025.* Retrieved from https://www.ets.org/content/dam/ets-org/pdfs/praxis/5025.pdf

Ehri, L. (1999). Phases of development in learning to read words. In J. Oakhill & R. Beard (Eds.), Reading Development and the Teaching of Reading: A Psychological Perspective, 79-108. Oxford, UK: Blackwell Publishers.

Gelman, R., & Gallistel, C. R. (1978). The Child's Understanding of Number. Cambridge, MA: Harvard University Press.

Heim, D. (2018). *The international dateline, explained.* LifeScience. Retrieved from https://www.livescience.com/44292-international-date-line-explained.html

Landt, S. M. (2006). Multicultural literature and young adolescents: A kaleidoscope of opportunity. *Journal of Adolescent & Adult Literacy*, 49(8), 690-697.

Lyon, G. R., & Moats, L. C. (1997). Critical Conceptual and Methodological Considerations in Reading Intervention Research. *Journal of Learning Disabilities*, 30(6), 578–588. https://doi.org/10.1177/002221949703000601

Mayer, K. (2007). Research in review: Emerging knowledge about emergent writing. Retrieved from http://resourcebinderecse.weebly.com/uplo

Merriam Webster (2019). Nation - Definition. Retrieved from https://www.merriam-webster.com/dictionary/nation

Merriam Webster (2019). Paraphrase - Definition. Retrieved from https://www.merriam-webster.com/dictionary/paraphrase

Merriam Webster (2019). Plagiarize - Definition. Retrieved from https://www.merriam-webster.com/dictionary/plaigarize

NASA (n.d.). *Earth. Solar system exploration.* Retrieved from https://solarsystem.nasa.gov/planets/earth/in-depth/

NASA (n.d.). *Newton's Laws of Motion.* Retrieved from https://www.grc.nasa.gov/www/k-12/airplane/newton.html

NASA (n.d.). *Our solar system.* Retrieved from https://solarsystem.nasa.gov/solar-system/our-solar-system/overview/

National Geographic (n.d.). *Continental drift.* Retrieved from https://www.nationalgeographic.org/encyclopedia/continental-drift/

National Geographic (n.d.). *Ecological relationships.* Retrieved from https://www.nationalgeographic.org/activity/ecological-relationships/

National Geographic (n.d.). *Geography.* National Geographic: Resource Library. Retrieved from https://www.nationalgeographic.org/encyclopedia/geography/

National Geographic (n.d.). *Hemisphere*. National Geographic: Resource Library. Retrieved from https://www.nationalgeographic.org/encyclopedia/hemisphere/

National Oceanic and Atmospheric Administration (NOAA) (2019). *What is a tsunami?* Retrieved from https://oceanservice.noaa.gov/facts/tsunami.html

National Oceanic and Atmospheric Administration. (n.d.). *Stratospheric ozone.* Retrieved from https://www.ozonelayer.noaa.gov/science/basics.htm

National Research Council (2012). *A framework for k-12 science education: Practices, crosscutting concepts, and core ideas.* Washington, DC: The National Academies Press. https://doi.org/10.17226/13165.

National Severe Storms Laboratory (NSSL) (2019). *Lightning basics.* https://www.nssl.noaa.gov/education/svrwx101/lightning/

Philpott, D. (2003). Sovereignty. In *Stanford Encyclopedia of Philosophy.* Retrieved from https://plato.stanford.edu/entries/sovereignty/

Piaget, J. (1975). *The equilibration of cognitive structure.* Chicago, IL: University of Chicago Press.

Pidwirny, M. (2006). Organization of life: species, populations, communities, and ecosystems. *Fundamentals of Physical Geography, 2nd Edition.* Date Viewed. http://www.physicalgeography.net/fundamentals/9d.html

Shioshita, J. (1997). Beyond good intentions: Selecting multicultural literature. *Children's Advocate* newsmagazine.

Temming, M (2014). What is a star? *Sky and telescope.* Retrieved from https://www.skyandtelescope.com/astronomy-resources/what-is-a-star/

The White House (n.d.). State and local government. Retrieved from: https://www.whitehouse.gov/about-the-white-house/state-local-government/

Vygotsky,L.S. (1978) *Mind in society: The development of higher psychological processes.* London: Harvard University Press.

Whitehurst, G., & Lonigan, C. (1998). Child Development and Emergent Literacy. *Child Development, 69*(3), 848-872. doi:10.2307/1132208

Made in the USA
Columbia, SC
04 January 2025

51229469R00115